CAMBRIDGE SKILLS FOR FLUENCY
Series Editor: Adrian Doff

Cheng Kam-kit

Speaking 3

Joanne Collie
Stephen Slater

Hobson's choice
— no choice

May I know your Name? (too formal).
What's your name?
I'm ___ and you are ___?
your name is ___?

Synonym — same meaning.

'ish' (about)
twenty - ish.
Are you hungry (ish)

CAMBRIDGE
UNIVERSITY PRESS

PUBLISHED BY THE PRESS SYNDICATE OF THE UNIVERSITY OF CAMBRIDGE
The Pitt Building, Trumpington Street, Cambridge, United Kingdom

CAMBRIDGE UNIVERSITY PRESS
The Edinburgh Building, Cambridge CB2 2RU, UK
40 West 20th Street, New York, NY 10011–4211, USA
477 Williamstown Road, Port Melbourne, VIC 3207, Australia
Ruiz de Alarcón 13, 28014 Madrid, Spain
Dock House, The Waterfront, Cape Town 8001, South Africa

http://www.cambridge.org

First published 1992
Tenth printing 2002

Printed in the United Kingdom at the University Press, Cambridge

ISBN 0 521 39970 X book
ISBN 0 521 39971 8 cassette

GO

Contents

Jane   How long does it take you to get home from B.C.?

a couple of / hours
few

How old were you when you started learning English?

Map of the book

Unit	Themes/Vocabulary areas	Areas of communication	Learner activities
1	Gifts, tickets and travel, phones, thanking people.	Discussing personal memories; relating anecdotes; expressing reactions and thanks.	Listening and note-taking; role-play; listening and reacting; planning and giving a short speech.
2	Personal appearance, changes in appearance.	Discussing appearance; comparing reactions and opinions; explaining likes and dislikes.	Questionnaire; making and justifying choices in groups; interviewing; pair discussion.
3	Dances, attitudes to dancing, Morris dancing.	Responding to music; reminiscing; comparing folk traditions.	Listening and matching; listening and reacting; guessing and listening in pairs; creating a dance.
4	Smells and what they evoke; perfumes, aftershave, advertisements; aromatherapy.	Describing smells; comparing personal reactions and memories; exchanging ideas.	Groupwork with a questionnaire; writing profiles; creating a radio programme; reading and discussion.
5	Jewellery, precious stones, family heirlooms.	Talking about ornaments; describing rooms and possessions; talking about future events.	Listening, pair matching, pyramid discussion; making lists and guessing in groups; discussion in pairs.
6	Cities, urban conditions and problems, beggars.	Comparing features, reporting information, exchanging views; supporting arguments.	Making lists; interviewing others, note-taking, oral reports; listening and retelling stories in groups, organising a three-person debate.
7	Self-defence, danger and violence in cities.	Comparing opinions and experiences; reacting to and discussing a threatening situation.	Finding others with same/different views; group reactions to a hypothetical situation; writing in pairs; listening.
8	Being helped and helping others, emergency situations, help for the underprivileged, help in learning English.	Talking about problems, personal preferences; summarising discussions; answering queries; analysing learning strategies.	Listening in pairs to confirm guesses; group ranking of problems and reporting to others; questionnaire; preparation of a spoken report.
9	Success in life, recorded advice.	Talking about, giving and assessing advice, sharing opinions and reactions.	Pair ranking activity; listening and matching; group preparation of a recorded message.

Unit	Themes/Vocabulary areas	Areas of communication	Learner activities
10	Walking, jogging, weight control, fitness, unusual sports, fun walks.	Discussing personal choices, opinions; exchanging information; negotiating a group activity.	Guessing in pairs; matching; interviewing; statement completion in pairs; class project; organising a fun walk.
11	The human kidneys, moral issues relating to organ transplants.	Checking facts; justifying moral stances; negotiating decisions; advising; continuing a narrative.	Answering a questionnaire; group discussion of social issues; mini simulation; feedback; listening.
12	Gambling and attitudes to it.	Comparing personal and national attitudes; talking about experiences and personality.	Class game of chance; discussion; groupwork with a questionnaire; vocabulary work; listening and retelling; group questionnaire and discussion.
13	Making risky decisions in life, mutiny, obeying difficult instructions.	Talking about a historical event; making a decision; negotiating a group activity or observing and reporting.	Group discussion of a visual; guided fantasy – simulation; feedback.
14	Films, film stars, TV, video, attitudes to TV, reading.	Comparing guesses; making and sharing decisions; negotiating.	Group guessing game and feedback; listening and note-taking, pair exchange of views; pairwork on a questionnaire; making choices in groups; class project outside classroom.
15	'Soaps' – storyline and characters in television serials.	Seeking and sharing information and opinions.	Conducting interviews; pooling results; guided script writing project and performance.
16	Pets, attitudes to animals, bird migrations, human sense of direction.	Exchanging and sharing knowledge; expressing and justifying opinions.	Pairwork vocabulary grid; listening, note-taking, information gathering and sharing, group discussion.
17	Dangerous dogs, attacks on humans, coping with this problem.	Exchanging views on social problems; discussing options; making and justifying decisions in a hypothetical situation.	Small group discussion; indicating opinions by standing on a line; mini simulation; group discussion and feedback.
18	Neighbours, good and bad, changes in neighbourhoods; neighbouring countries.	Finding out and discussing differences of opinion; talking about past experiences; describing places and changes; negotiating views about countries.	Pairwork with a questionnaire; group vocabulary work and discussion; listening; creating an imaginary map; feedback.
19	Disputes between neighbours, ideas of revenge.	Imagining and discussing a hypothetical situation; reacting to changes, making and justifying decisions.	Guided simulation in groups based on ongoing listening prompts; group and class discussion.
20	Memorials and what they mean.	Exchanging views on a historical site and on one's own town; commenting on the learning material used in this book.	Pair discussion of a visual; writing an ending to a story and relating it; listening to confirm guesses; pair vocabulary work; preparation of a short tourist cassette guide; individual commentary on this book.

Acknowledgements

The authors and publishers would like to thank the following teachers and institutions which piloted *Speaking 3* for us. Without their constructive suggestions, the improvements in the book would not have been made:
Kevin Forde, British Council, Hong Kong; Norma Innes, Lilliput Language Centre, Poole; Sean Power, ASC Language Training, Geneva.

The authors and publishers are grateful to the following individuals and institutions for permission to reproduce copyright material:
NSP Catalogue Holdings plc (p. 3); Barnaby's Picture Library (pp. 7 judge, 11, 37, 51 – pictures 3 and 5, 54); Sally and Richard Greenhill Photolibrary (p. 7 woman having hair permed, clown, man with tattoo, barrister, 14, 23, 25, 29, 31); Tony Stone Worldwide (p. 9 A); Society for Cultural Relations with the USSR (p. 9, B); J Allan Cash (p. 9 C; p. 75) Pratap and Priya Pawar, Kathak dancers of the Triveni dance company, photograph by Vinod Verma (p. 9 D); All Media Services, Eurocos Cosmetic, Lansdown Euro Ltd., Nina Ricci, for advertisements (p. 15); Mechanical Copyright Protection Society for the music to *Lean on me*; International Music Publications: *Lean on me* lyrics by Bill Withers © 1972 Interior Music Inc USA, EMI Music Publishing Ltd, London WC2H 0EA (p. 29); Trade and Travel Publications for the map of São Paulo taken from the *South American Handbook 1992* (p. 39); Lonely Planet Publications for the map of Harare taken from *Africa on a shoestring* by Geoff Crowther and the map of Tokyo from *Japan – a travel survival kit* by Ian McQueen (p. 39); Department of Health for the donor card (p. 41); The National Maritime Museum (p. 48); The Kobal Collection (p. 51 – pictures 1, 2, 4 and 6).

Thanks also to students at Eurocentres, Cambridge and to staff at Centre 33, Cambridge for taking part in photographs.
The photographs on pp. 1, 22, 27, 32, 63, 64 and 73 were taken by Jeremy Pembrey and on p. 7 person with glasses, pp. 38, 44, 45, 49 and 56 by Adrian Evans and Joanne Bexley.
Drawings by Chris Evans (pp. 2, 10, 18, 24, 69, 77); Leslie Marshall (pp. 13, 19, 36, 44, 59, 76); Chris Rothero (pp. 17, 46); Chris Pavely (pp. 26, 57, 58); Shaun Williams (pp. 33); Lisa Hall (pp. 43, 71); Joanne Slater (p. 52); Steve Lings (pp. 60–61); Stephen Slater (p. 70).
Artwork by Hardlines and Peter Ducker.
Book design by Peter Ducker MSTD.

1 | A dozen red potatoes

Giving and receiving presents

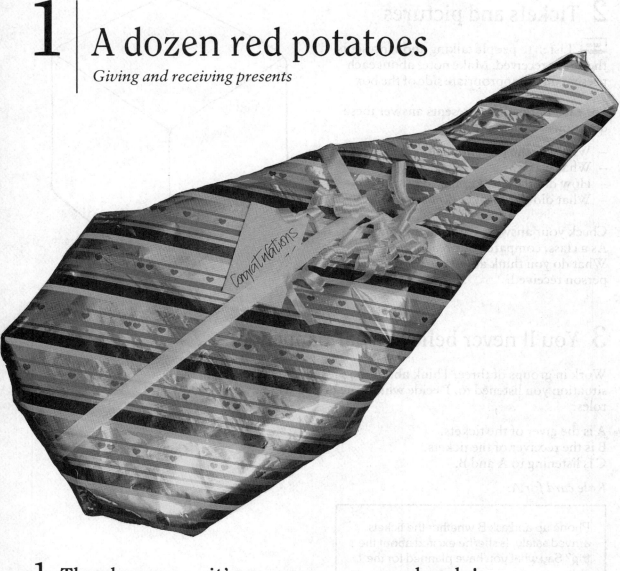

1 Thank you . . . it's . . . . er . . . . lovely!

With another student guess what the present in the photo might be.

Do you have any memories of these kinds of presents:
- unusual presents
- presents that you really liked
- presents that you remember for some special reason
- presents that seemed ridiculous
- presents that you wanted to throw away

In small groups, tell each other about these memories.

2 Tickets and pictures

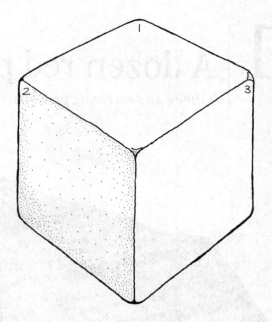

Listen to people talking about presents they have received. Make notes about each present on the appropriate side of the box.

For each of the three presents answer these questions:

- Who was the present from?
- What was it?
- How did the speaker feel about it?
- What did the speaker do with it?

Check your answers with other groups.
As a class, compare your reactions.
What do you think about the presents each person received?

3 You'll never believe what happened . . .

Work in groups of three. Think about the present of the tickets, in the last situation you listened to. Decide which one of you will have the following roles:

A is the giver of the tickets.
B is the receiver of the tickets.
C is listening to A and B.

Role card for A:

> Phone up and ask B whether the tickets arrived safely. Is she/he excited about the trip? Say what you have planned for the visit.

Role card for B:

> Your teacher will give you and C a slip of paper to tell you what happened next. Read it. When A phones you up, answer her/his questions. Are you going to tell the truth?

Task for C:

> Listen to the telephone conversation
> between A and B. Tell them your reaction
> to what happened. Do you agree with the
> way B talked about the situation?

You can change roles and role-play a phone call for one of the other two
situations you listened to.
Instead of being given a slip of paper, B and C decide together what
happened next.

4 Quack, quack . . . quack, quack . . . Can you answer that, please?

Duck Phones

These delightful new duck
phones are made from
wood and are hand painted.
They make a wonderful
change from standard
phones.
    They don't ring, they
quack! And the eyes light
up when you use the phone.

Would this duck phone make a good present for someone you know?
Why . . . or why not? Talk to another student about it.

We showed three people the ad and asked them the same question. Can you
guess what they said?

Listen to the cassette and with your partner, find at least two reasons for
giving or not giving the duck phone as a present.
See whether others have picked out the same reasons.
Do you agree with any of the speakers?

5 Thank you so much for the lovely . . .

Someone is leaving your English class next week and moving to another town. The other students in the class are going to give this person a present. Work in pairs. Assume everyone in the class has contributed a small amount of money. Follow these three stages:

1 Decide what present to buy. (Write the names of two possible gifts on two separate slips of paper and give them to your teacher.)
2 When your teacher has collected all the slips and put them in a box, choose one slip of paper each. Imagine that you are the student who is leaving, and see what gift the class has given you.
3 Now, prepare a short speech to say thank you to the class for the present. Imagine it is your last day in class.

With your partner, talk about the things you could say in your speech. You know what gift you have received, so think about these questions:

— Were you surprised to receive it?
— How will you use the gift?
— Where will you put it?
— Is it an especially suitable gift for your situation?
— Is it a present that you will remember? Why?

Prepare your speech, either in class or at home.

Sit in small groups. In turn, practise your speeches together. Give each other helpful comments. One or two of you might like to make your speech to the class.

2 | Judging by appearances

Personal appearance

1 Shall I bother?

Work with a partner. Fill in this questionnaire for yourself, by circling the right letter. Then, without asking her or him, fill it in for your partner, by putting a tick next to the appropriate letter.
When you have finished compare your answers.

---

1 **A close friend asks you round for coffee. You:**
   a) go as you are.
   b) wash and tidy yourself up, then go.
   c) wash, tidy yourself up, change your clothes, then go.

2 **You've been painting. A friend rings up, wanting some help with an emergency in the house. You:**
   a) go immediately, as you are.
   b) wash your hands quickly and go.
   c) wash quickly, change your clothes, then go.

3 **You've decided to go on a special holiday to a warm seaside place. You:**
   a) plan what to do but not what to wear.
   b) plan what to wear and buy new clothes.
   c) think about your appearance, go on a diet, do exercises to be fit and look well.

4 **Your boss asks you to go to an important meeting. You:**
   a) wash and tidy yourself up but don't wear anything special.
   b) wear your best clothes and make sure you're neat and tidy.
   c) go out and buy some expensive new clothes.

5 **You have to go for a job interview. You:**
   a) are neat but look much as you do every day.
   b) wear your best clothes and make sure you are neat and tidy.
   c) have a haircut or hairdo, buy new clothes.

6 **You're about to go out to your English class when you notice a food stain on the front of your clothes. You:**
   a) put your jacket over it and hope it won't show.
   b) try to get rid of it by scrubbing.
   c) change your clothes.

7 **You get up late for work. Your clothes are clean but not ironed. You:**
   a) put them on and hope the creases won't show.
   b) choose something else to wear even if it's not quite right for the weather.
   c) take the time to iron.

Talk about your answers with another pair. How much effort do you think should be put into appearance?
When is it important to make a special effort?

2 All you really need is a big smile

Here are some factors which may be important for appearance. In a small
group, add any others that you think are important.

clean hair   clean clothes   clean shoes

new clothes   fashionable clothes   informal clothes

bright jewellery   expensive jewellery   one piece of jewellery only

a big smile   a friendly expression   a serious expression

a straight back   a relaxed attitude

bright eyes   white teeth   strong shoulders   long legs

Others _____

_____

In your group, choose the three most important factors for these people.
Add two other kinds of people to the list.

	Three important factors		
a politician	....	....	....
a teacher	....	....	....
a hitch-hiker	....	....	....
a salesperson	....	....	....
a	....	....	....
a	....	....	....

Compare your choices with other pairs. What thoughts helped you to make
your choices?

3 Appearances can be deceptive

In groups of three or four, write numbers from 1 to 7 on slips of paper and
put them into a container. In turn, pick a number. Look in the key at the
statement corresponding to that number. Say why you think it is generally
true, or generally false.
See whether others in the group agree with you.

Now play the game again. Add slips of paper numbered 8, 9 and 10. If you
pick numbers 8, 9 or 10, you must make up a statement about appearance,
and say why you think it is generally true or false.

4 Changing appearance

How many ways are there of changing or disguising your appearance?
With a partner, list as many as you can. Then choose at least two and write
notes about them using these ideas:

Reason for the change?
Effects on personality?
When is it useful?
When is it harmful?

Join another pair and talk about the changes you chose and your ideas about
them.

5 I just can't stand . . .

I can't stand women with heavy makeup.

I know it's unreasonable but bald people make me squirm!

I can't get used to men with earrings.

Well, personally, I've never liked redheads.

No, I hate moustaches or beards

False eyelashes are horrible!

People who are very thin just aren't for me.

(add your own)

What particular appearances do you dislike? Choose one of the comments, or jot down one of your own. Interview the other students in your class about their pet hates, and tell them about your own. Is there someone else in the class who has the same dislikes as you do?

3 | Rhythm and blues

Dances and dancing

A

1 Dances of the world

B

C

D

With another student, look at these pictures. Do you know what kind of dance each picture shows?

Listen to four pieces of dance music. Decide which picture goes with which piece.

Compare your answers with other pairs. Has anyone in your class ever done any of these dances? Which would you like to try?

2 The last time I went dancing . . .

▭ Listen to two people talking about the last time they went dancing. Note down the style of dancing they describe, and how they felt about the situation.

	Style of dancing	*How did they feel?*
Person 1		
Person 2		

With one or two others talk about the last time you went dancing. Was it like the stories on the cassette?

— Where did you dance?
— Who were you with?
— Why did you go?
— How did you feel?
— Were you a good dancer?

Is there anyone in the group who has never done any dancing at all? Compare your experiences.

3 My feet just start tapping . . .

What kind of music makes you want to dance?

▭ Listen to these four pieces of music. Which one do you prefer?

Find another student who made a different choice from yours. Talk about the kind of dancing you like best.
Do you prefer to dance yourself or to watch other people dancing?

4 Morris dancing

These are objects which are used in a traditional English dance called Morris dancing. Do you know how they are used and what they mean? Ask other students and see how much the class as a whole knows about them.

Now listen to an English person talking about the objects.
Were your guesses about them right?

What folk dances or regional dances do you have in your country?
If you are all from one country, see how many you can list.
If you are from different countries, talk about your own country's dances with some other students. Are any objects used in them? Is there a special musical instrument for the dances?

5 Dances to make things happen

This picture shows a dance to make the rain fall. Are there any dances to make things happen in your folklore?

Sit in a small group. Together, decide on one thing or event you really want (having a lovely holiday by the seaside, winning a lottery, etc.).
Think of a simple dance 'to make it happen'. Talk about movements or gestures to symbolise the event.

Get together with another group. Perform or describe your dance for each other.
Can you guess the thing or event the other group wants?

11

4 | A garden of roses

Smells, perfumes, aromatherapy

1 Roses and rubbish heaps

Tick the letter that is the closest to your ideas or feelings:

1 When I think of marvellous smells, I think particularly of:
   a) people.
   c) places.
   b) flowers.
   d) food or drink.

2 When I think of terrible smells, I think particularly of:
   a) people.
   c) places.
   b) food or drink.
   d) rubbish heaps.

3 I especially like the smell of:
   a) someone who has been exercising.
   c) a baby just washed.
   b) freshly baked bread.
   d) a spice market.

4 I like to think that I have:
   a) a fresh, natural smell.
   c) no smell at all.
   b) a light, fragrant smell.
   d) an alluring, sensual smell.

5 When I go into a home I like its smell to:
   a) tell me something about the people who live in it.
   b) be lightly fragrant — candles, perfumes...
   c) be new and clean.
   d) be spicy or heavily fragrant.

6 When I go into an office building I like it to have:
   a) a smell of papers and files.
   b) a fresh, natural smell.
   c) a smell of polish.
   d) a minty scent wafted through air conditioning.

Profiles:
Majority (a): You are ....
Majority (b): You are ....
Majority (c): You are ....
Majority (d): You are ....

In small groups, compare your results.

Here are some adjectives that could describe people who have a majority of
A's, B's, C's or D's.
Decide which ones are appropriate, and choose at least one for each of the
sentences in the profile above.

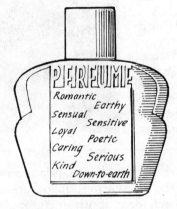

Consult other groups, and see whether you can all agree on one profile.

2 I remember . . .

With a partner, talk about these questions:

— How sensitive to smells are you?
— What smells can you remember from your childhood?
— What smells do you like best?
— What is the worst smell you can remember?

Make notes about your own experiences and those you hear about, then
change partners. Compare your notes with those of your new partner.

3 An interview programme

Read this preview article in the *Radio Journal*. It describes a programme that is to be broadcast.

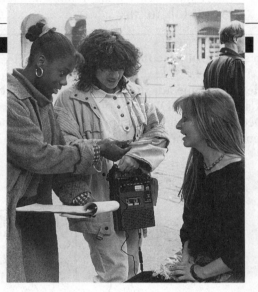

■ MAGDA BACK ON THE SCENT ■

On Wednesday 6 April, Magda Stevenson returns to Radio Seven with a new series of 'Magda Interviews' – this time she's been asking people about smells. It's not a subject we hear much about but most people have surprisingly strong views on the whole question, as Magda found out when she started talking to people on the street. One pensioner in Brighton still recalls vividly the smell of the wild thyme in Provence where she grew up over sixty years ago. And then there's the student in Edinburgh who discovered more than he bargained for when he investigated the curious smell coming from what seemed to be an abandoned shed . . . Listen in on Wednesday!

In groups of four or five, create a radio programme, like 'Magda Interviews', about smells. One member of the group is the interviewer, the others are people interviewed in the street. Use your own ideas about smell, or use the notes you made in Activity 2. If you can, record your programme. Present your radio programme to the class.

4 Perfumes and aftershave

Look at the advertisements opposite. What qualities do the companies want the reader to associate with their perfumes and aftershave lotions?

immense space   a lively life   colour and fun   sexual attraction
a light happy feeling   heavy passion   others: ....
....

In small groups, compare your feelings about these ads, and about these questions:
— Do you feel we try to cover our body smell too much by using perfumes or cosmetics?
— Do you think it is dangerous to use perfumes and let chemicals be absorbed into the body?

If you can, bring in other examples of advertisements from magazines or newspapers that you read.

Discuss each ad and give it a rating from 0 to 5 for each of the following categories:

☐ Aesthetic quality   (Do I like the look of the ad?
                                0 = No, it's ugly   5 = Yes, it's beautiful)

☐ Effectiveness   (Does it make me want to buy the product?
                                0 = Definitely not   5 = Yes, definitely)

☐ ....   (Add your own criterion if you wish)

Organise an exhibition of ads brought in by different groups in the class, including the group's assessment. Other people can agree or disagree with the group's assessment.

5 Air conditioned response?

FRAGRANCE can have a positive effect on our moods, according to a Japanese company, Shimizu, who circulate mood-enhancing aromatherapy oils through air conditioning systems in their offices. Studies show that environmental fragrancing has an uplifting effect on the mind and body. After exposure to lavender, jasmine and lemon scents, efficiency levels and alertness during meetings increased, and typing errors were reduced. Now specific fragrances are used to good effect in hotels, retirement homes and hospitals in Japan: lemon to energise, jasmine to relax and lavender and peppermint to curb the urge to smoke. You can create your own mood fragrances. Leading aromatherapist Sheilagh Neil suggests placing a tissue impregnated with oil into the air vent of your car. At home, try placing a dish of essential oil near a warm radiator.

With one or two other students, discuss this article. Consider these questions:

— Do you agree that fragrances have an uplifting effect on people?
— Do you agree with the practice of using fragrances in the workplace? (Say why or why not.)
— Do you use aromatherapy in your home?
— If so, what effect does it have?
— If not, would you like to try? (Say why or why not.)

5 | Rings on my fingers and bells on my toes

Jewellery, ornaments and family treasures

1 I never go anywhere without it

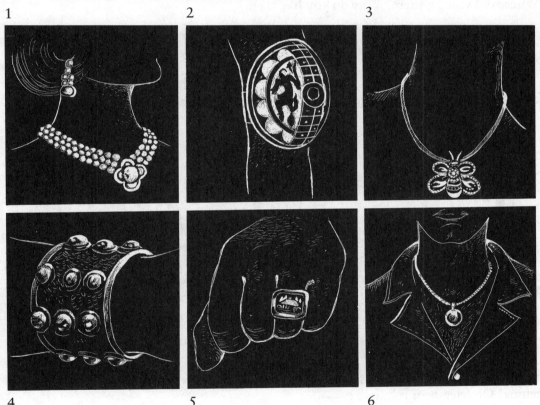

1 2 3

4 5 6

Listen to four people talking about their favourite piece of jewellery. With another student, match each speaker with one of the pictures above.

Speaker 1: .... Speaker 3: ....

Speaker 2: .... Speaker 4: ....

Check your answers with another pair. With them, talk about each of these ornaments. Which are popular in your own country?

2 Where did you get that ring?

In a group of three or four students, look at the visible personal ornaments each of you is wearing at this moment.

How many:

rings	....	things to wear around the neck	....
watches	....	brooches or pins	....
badges of any kind	....	bracelets	....
others	....		

Do any of them have a special meaning for you?
Tell the others any interesting facts about these ornaments or others that you have. Where did you get them? Why do you like them?

3 Precious stones

Can you match the appropriate colours with these precious stones?

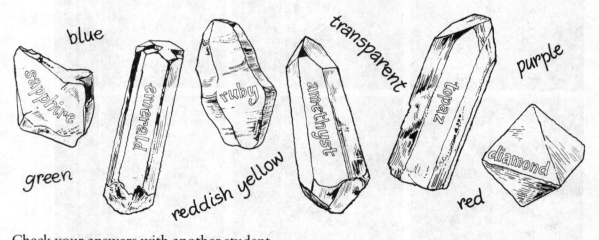

Check your answers with another student.

How many of these precious stones have you seen? Where did you see them?
In museums? On friends or relatives?
Which precious stones are popular in your country?

Sometimes precious stones are associated with certain powers. For example, some people believe that:

– the opal brings bad luck
– the aquamarine brings good luck to sailors
– the amethyst has supernatural powers

Are there any beliefs of this kind about precious stones in your country?

Precious stones are also associated with birthdays. As a class, try this experiment. Write down on a slip of paper the precious stone you like best. After you have done this, check the list of birthstones in the key. How many people in your class chose their own birthstone?

In small groups, choose a precious stone to represent your English class. Can the class agree on one choice?

4 It belonged to my grandfather

With another student, take it in turns to describe one or two of the main rooms in a house or flat you know well – your own, your parents' or another relative's.

In particular, talk about things in each room which have been passed down from previous generations of the family.

They could be:

– ornaments (vases, pottery, porcelain figurines . . .)
– pictures (oil, water colours, etchings, photos . . .)
– furniture (tables, chairs, desks . . .)
– newspaper cuttings, books, poems . . .
– jewellery, musical instruments . . .
– other items: ....

Who did the items belong to originally? When did your family receive them? Which ones do you like most and why?

Would you like to have more things from previous generations of your family? What things and why? Or . . . why not?

5 I want you to have my . . .

List some items which belong to you and which you care about – either because they are worth a lot of money or because they have great sentimental value.

Worth a lot of money	*Of great sentimental value*
....	....
....	....
....	....
....	....

Talk about some of the items on your lists with one or two other students.

What is going to happen to these items when you die? Are you going to give them to charity or leave them to family or friends?
Complete some of these sentences, using items from your lists.

I'm going to leave my .... to ....

I'm going to take my .... with me when I die.

I'm going to give my .... to .... before I die.

I'm not going to leave anything, I'm going to sell my ....
before I die and have a good time with the money I get for it.

I'm going to burn my ....

Now take it in turns to read out the names of the items in your sentences to another student. Can your partner guess what you are planning to do with each item?

6 | Concrete jungles?

Towns and cities

1 Cities of the world

Look at this list of cities. How many of them have you been to?

Tokyo
New York
Rome
London
Singapore
Cairo
Rio de Janeiro

Jakarta
Toronto
Sydney
Istanbul
Los Angeles
Paris
Amsterdam

Buenos Aires
Madrid
Calcutta
Beijing
Lagos
Auckland

Add other cities if you like: ....

Choose:
— three cities you would like to live in:

....

— three cities you would hate to live in:

....

In small groups, talk about your lists. What particular aspects made you
choose these cities?

2 Favourite corners

Many people who live in
towns or cities have favourite
places in them – little corner
shops or outdoor markets,
local restaurants, quiet
squares, parks . . .

Interview two other people in
the class. Ask them questions
about the city they come from.

Find out:
– where their favourite place is
– how often they go there,
  and whether they go alone
  or with friends
– what things they like about it
– what kind of people they
  meet there
– how long they have known it

Make notes, then prepare an oral report.

Sit with two or three other students and take it in turns to give your reports
to the group.

3 How safe is this town or city?

With your group, talk about the town or city in which you are living at the
moment.
How safe or dangerous do you think it is?
Are there parts of the town or city that are unsafe to walk in alone at night?
Is the city or town becoming more dangerous than it used to be? If you are
new to the city or town, ask some locals this question.

Compare your views with those of other students. Do men and women have
different opinions on these questions?

4 What an experience!

📼 Sit with two partners. Listen to three people talking about experiences they have had in cities.
Each one of you is responsible for taking notes on what one of the speakers says. Make sure you take notes about:

— the city that each speaker is talking about
— what happened, if anything
— their reaction

When you have listened to all three, try to retell the story on which you took notes. Compare the experiences of the three speakers.

5 Beggars

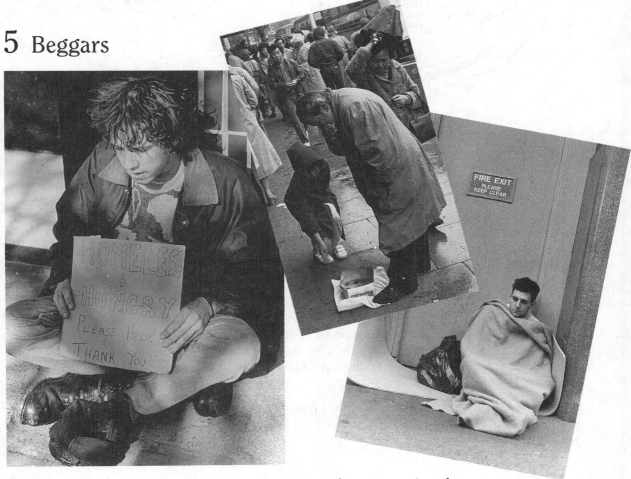

Beggars are a feature of many cities. Are there any in the town or city where you live?
If so, where? Are they threatening? Do you believe in giving money to them?
If not, have you met any in other cities? How did you feel about that?

⋙→

Talk about the following questions with another student. What is your attitude generally? Are your views closer to A, to B, or to C?

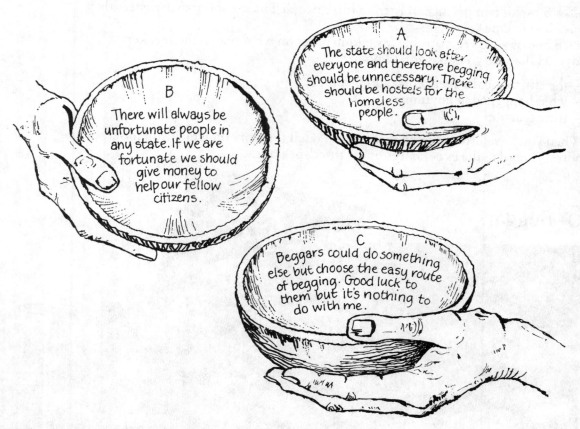

Find other students whose views are similar to your own.

If the class is divided in its views:
Form three groups of people with similar views. Discuss the problem of begging and prepare arguments to support your views.
Then organise a three-cornered debate. One member from each group gives the arguments prepared. After the three people have spoken, people can question any of the groups.

If most people in the class have the same views:
Form small groups and discuss the problem of begging. Can you think of any solution to the problem?

7 | Dangerous situations

Self defence and coping with danger

1 Self defence

Are you able to defend yourself in a dangerous situation?

YES	NO
If your answer is yes, find a student who also said yes, and discuss how you defend yourself.	If your answer is no, find a student who also said no and discuss what you would do in a dangerous situation.
Have you studied some form of martial art, like karate?	Would you run away? . . . try to talk your way out of danger? . . . shout for help?
Did you learn how to fight and defend yourself as a child?	Have you ever studied some form of martial art, like karate?
Are you physically strong?	Do you carry anything, like a whistle, in case of emergencies?
Have you had to defend yourself recently?	Have you been in a dangerous situation recently?

Now change partners. If you are a 'yes', talk with a 'no' and compare your reactions to these questions.
What about your teacher?

2 Why does he keep staring at me?

These two people are standing at a bus stop. Why does the woman feel uncomfortable? In small groups, discuss possible reasons.

Now imagine that the two people have to wait several more minutes. What do you think happens next?

a) The woman walks quickly away to another bus stop.
b) The woman says: 'Terrible bus service, isn't it!'
c) The woman says: 'Why are you staring at me?'
d) The man says: 'Terrible bus service, isn't it!'
e) Other: ....

Compare your choices. Discuss what the two people do and say. What are they thinking? Their thoughts may be very different from their words and actions.

3 Bus stop

In pairs, take the roles of the two people. Imagine that you are at a quiet bus stop in your own town or city. Prepare a short scene to show what could happen.

Here is another way of presenting the scene. Work in groups of four. One student takes the part of the man and another plays the woman. They stand at the bus stop and they can talk or not talk. The other two students stand close behind and speak the thoughts of the man and the woman.

4 Got a light?

Sit with three other students. Imagine this situation:

> You are walking along a dark city street at night. You are alone. You suddenly hear footsteps behind you and a voice calls out.

Listen to the voice and in your group, talk about your first reaction to this situation.

What would you do?
How would you feel?
What would you say?

Now imagine that the situation continues.

> The man has not gone away. He is unshaven but he is quite well dressed.

Listen to what the man says next. There is no one else in the street. With your group, decide what to do and say now.

⟫⟫→

The situation continues.

> The man still has not gone away, and he is now
> starting to get impatient.

🔲 Listen to what he says. Discuss the choices that you now have. What is the best thing to do and say? Why? Do you all agree?

> No matter what you do or say, the man will not go
> away. He is getting angry.

🔲 Listen to what he says. In your group talk about your feelings at this point. What are you going to do now?

Imagine how the situation continues after this. How does it end? Together, think of possibilities.

5 Something like this happened to . . .

As a class, talk about the situation you have just listened to and discussed. Has anything like this ever happened to anyone in the class, or anyone you know?
Have you ever been frightened when you were out at night?
Have you ever been attacked?
Has someone you know been attacked?

Tell your story to the others in the class.

8 | Lean on me

Helping others

1 Lean on me

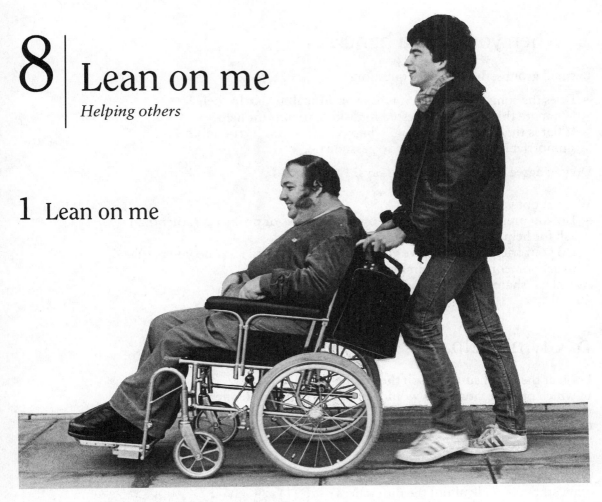

With another student, read the words to the song 'Lean on me'. Try to fill in the gaps in the text.
Compare your guesses with those of other students.

> Sometime in our lives we all have pain, we all have ....
> But if we are .... , we know that there's always tomorrow.
> Lean on me when you're not ....
> And I'll be your .... , I'll help you carry on
> For it won't be long, till I'm going to ....
> Somebody to lean on.
>
> Please swallow your .... if I have faith you need to borrow
> For no one can fill those of your needs that you won't let show.
> You just call on me brother, when you need a ....
> We all need somebody to lean on.
> I just might have a .... that you'll understand
> We all need somebody to lean on.

Now listen to the song and see if your guesses were correct.

2 When you need a hand . . .

In small groups, discuss these questions:

— Does the song suggest that it is easy or difficult to ask for help?
— What are the reasons suggested for asking friends for help?
— What is the mood of the song: happy?   sad?   friendly?
   supportive?   optimistic?   pessimistic?

Do you agree with what the song says?

What about yourself?
— Do you prefer to work out your own difficulties or problems rather than
   ask for help?
— Do your friends usually give you help when you need it, or do you prefer
   to ask someone in your family?
As a class, share your views on these questions.

3 Giving help

Look at the list of situations in the box below.
In which of these situations would you find it easy to offer help, and in which
would you find it difficult?
Give each situation a score from 1 to 6:
(EASY FOR ME TO HELP) 1 .... 2 .... 3 .... 4 .... 5 .... 6 (IMPOSSIBLE FOR ME TO HELP)

Compare your scores with one or two
other students. Talk about the differences
between you and the reasons for those
differences. Which of these descriptions
best describes you?

I am . . .
— too helpful for my own good.
— reasonably helpful.
— too cautious to be very helpful.
— too scared to help in most situations.
— I've never had to give help so I just don't
   know.

Would you like to be more, or less helpful?
What would help you to change?
Report your thoughts and ideas to the rest
of the class.

☐	a very bad road accident
☐	someone who is being attacked in the street
☐	an injured snake
☐	a child (not your own!) who is lost and crying
☐	a pregnant woman who is about to have her baby
☐	someone who is threatening to jump out of a window
☐	an epileptic who is having a fit
☐	a drunk in the street

4 We should give more help to . . .

With a partner, think about your society. Which categories of people in this list deserve the most help in your country? Talk about this, then choose one or two of the groups from the list as your top priorities, or add other categories of your own.

children	the homeless	the sick	the uneducated
the poor	the elderly	the rich	the unemployed

Together, prepare a short spoken report on your discussion. Say which categories you have chosen and why. Make your report to another group. Answer their questions and respond to their comments.

5 Lean on your English teacher?

You are learning English. Some of your learning takes place in the classroom, but you do some of your learning on your own, without a teacher to help. Think about your present situation. Make a list of the aspects of English that you still want to improve.

Choose one item from your list. In what ways can the teacher help you with it? In what ways can you help yourself?

Discuss your thoughts with another student and then with your teacher.

If you chose to discuss improving your spoken English, has this book helped you in any way? Write and tell us your thoughts, even if you don't think the book has helped.
Write to:
   Joanne Collie and Stephen Slater, c/o Cambridge University Press, The Edinburgh Building, Shaftesbury Road, Cambridge CB2 2RU, UK.

9 | Just dial this number . . .

Organising a telephone helpline

1 How to be a success in life

Here are a few ideas about how to be a success in life. With a partner, choose the three you think are most important – you can add your own if you prefer.

- Don't spend any time on things that are not important.
- Be yourself: don't try to be someone else.
- Get a better education.
- Decide what you want and concentrate on that.
- Make friends with important people.
- Spend time and money on your appearance.
- Don't be afraid of failing.
- Be relaxed.
- Think positively: turn your weaknesses into strengths.
- ....
- ....

Discuss your ideas with another pair. What advice would you give to someone who wanted to be a success in life?

2 Telephoning for advice

In many countries it is possible to dial a number and listen to a few minutes
of recorded advice on the telephone.

Listen to this recorded advice about how to be a success in life.
As you listen, look again at the list in the previous activity.
Tick the ideas that the speaker mentions on the cassette. Are they the same as
the ones you chose from the list? What other ideas in the recorded advice are
missing from the list?

3 Helpline

Imagine that your group is a company that records advice over the
telephone. Every month you record a new message for your listeners.
Talk about the problems that most people need help with and then choose a
subject for this month's message. Prepare a short message of advice on one of
these, or choose your own:

— how to learn (or teach) English
— how to survive in a foreign country
— how to make friends when you have just moved to a new town
— boyfriend/girlfriend problems

If you can, record your message on to a cassette. Remember to try to keep
your tone as friendly and cheerful as possible!

Join up with another group. In turns, play or say your message to the others.
What do you think of the advice in their message?

4 Feedback

If you like, play your message to others in the class. Have most people chosen the same kind of problem? Are there other problems that seem to you more important?

As a class, discuss your experience of preparing and listening to the telephone messages.
Do you like the idea of recorded advice? Why . . . or why not?

> I think it's terrible; it just shows that there's no personal contact between people any more.

> Some form of contact is better than none; and anyway, some people feel more comfortable if they don't have to say who they are.

10 | On the move
Exercise and fitness

1 Walking or jogging?

Walking is restful and gives me time to observe things	Jogging makes you feel great, I do it regularly
✓ walking is good – it's something I'll be able to do for most of my life.	Jogging is good and I do it when I have time.
If I go walking, I don't need to dress up in running gear. equipment	Jogging is OK, but every time I do it I get bored and my feet hurt.
Walking is something I can do all day in beautiful surroundings, like mountains and hills.	Jogging may be good for me, but I don't like punishing myself just to be healthier.
Walking is for weak people who are too lazy to get fit.	Jogging is not for me: I'd rather spend my time doing more interesting things.
I don't like walking at all, so I usually take the car.	Jogging can become an obsession and then it's dangerous. hooked on Can't stop
Walking? You must be joking!	Jogging? You must be joking!

Choose the one sentence from each list which is similar to your views on
walking and jogging. Then write down the two sentences from the lists that
you think the student opposite you has chosen.
Compare the guesses with the choices your partner actually made.
Which is the most popular in your class – walking or jogging?

Talk about your attitudes to regular exercise.
Is physical exercise overrated? Do people take it too seriously? Is it an
important key to health and fitness?

2 Dieting: a national sport?

Exercise is often considered important for weight control. With a partner, match the physical activities with the calories used up (per minute) in doing them.

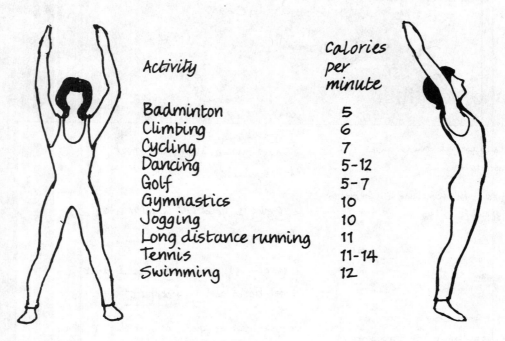

Activity	Calories per minute
Badminton	5
Climbing	6
Cycling	7
Dancing	5-12
Golf	5-7
Gymnastics	10
Jogging	10
Long distance running	11
Tennis	11-14
Swimming	12

What about your class? Is weight control a popular 'sport'? Interview other members and find out how many people:

- have never gone on a diet at all
- went on a diet to get thinner once only
- regularly go on diets to get thinner
- have gone on a diet to get fatter

It was not successful
I didn't succeed.

3 Moving in unusual ways

Look at this picture. Do you know what this sport is called? *Bungee Jumping*
Have you ever tried any unusual sport or activity?
With a partner complete each of these questions to create an interesting or
unusual ability, activity or sport. Then find another pair and ask them some
of your questions.

Can you walk on your _____ *Knees* _____ ?
Can you walk on a _____ *Cable wire* _____ ? *High wire (tighe-rope)*
Can you walk with a _____ *ball* _____ balanced on your head?
Can you ride a _____ *bull* _____ ?
Have you ever jumped from _____ *the roof* _____ ?
Have you ever climbed up _____ *the mount Everest* _____ ?
Can you _____ *lift up a car* _____ ?
Have you ever _____ *seen a ghost* _____ ?

Who seems to be the most unusual sportsperson in the room?

37

4 I prefer doing it my way!

With another student, talk about this picture. Is there anything unusual about it?

Now read this short text about Parlad Viranya and with your partner put in the missing words.

PARLAD VIRANYA from India started running .... after becoming tired of more conventional ways of running. He has .... 3126 miles from Los Angeles to New York, collecting money for charity. To .... him from colliding with things, Mr Viranya is accompanied by a navigator on a .... As a result, he has received few injuries, although his appearance often makes people.......................... He runs as fast as many long-distance forward runners, achieving speeds of up to 13 kilometres per hour.

What do you and your partner think about this way of raising money for charity? Can you think of other unusual ways that could be used?

5 Planning a fun walk

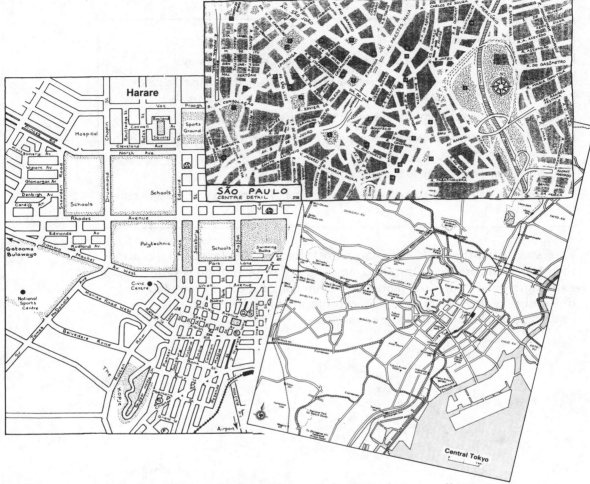

With one or two other students, talk about the total distance that you all believe you can comfortably walk in half an hour, or an hour.
When you have all agreed, start looking at a street map of your town, city or the area around your school.

Together plan a route that is interesting and varied, but one that doesn't have too many traffic problems. Make sure that the route is about equal to the total distance you agreed on. Discuss possible rest stops and any problems that you can think of.
Describe your route to other pairs, remembering to explain some of the reasons why you chose it.

Talk about the best date and starting time for your fun walk. Discuss what you might wear and how to carry any equipment (camera, drinks, note pads, etc.).

If you decide to carry out the fun walk, choose one task for each pair from the list below. Talk about your choices so that different people in the class are doing different things.

A Take three unusual photos.

B Make three sketches or rapid drawings of things you see on your way.

C Stop and talk to two people you see during your walk – find out and note down two interesting things about them.

D Find three interesting things and bring them back to the classroom.

E Note down details of three different leaves or flowers from interesting or unusual plants you see.

F Note down details of three animals or birds you see.

G Find three interesting examples of language (your own language or English) – note them down.

Feedback: After the walk, each pair reports back to the class and talks about their tasks, any problems they had, any unusual or memorable events. Pairs can prepare a written report of the fun walk for other groups to read, or for display. If you can, set up an exhibition of interesting photos, drawings, objects and language examples.

11 | The gift of life
Kidneys and transplants

1 What do you know about kidneys?

What do you know about kidneys? With a partner, see how many of the following questions you can answer:

1 Is a human kidney about the same size as a plum or bigger?

2 For how long (approximately) can a healthy human kidney be stored before it is transplanted?

    a) 6 hours   b) 24 hours   c) 3 months

3 When a kidney transplant is performed, where is the 'new' kidney put in the body?

4 How long does the average kidney transplant operation take?

    a) 1–2 hours   b) 3–4 hours   c) 5–6 hours

5 What is the function of the kidney in the body?

Find another pair and compare your answers.

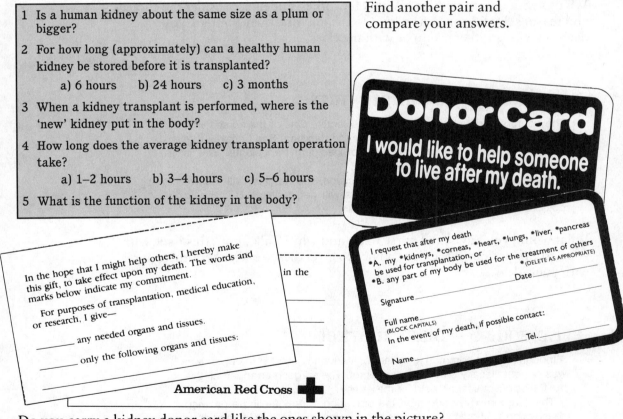

Donor Card
I would like to help someone to live after my death.

I request that after my death
*A. my *kidneys, *corneas, *heart, *lungs, *liver, *pancreas
be used for transplantation, or
*B. any part of my body be used for the treatment of others
    * (DELETE AS APPROPRIATE)

Date _____

Signature _____

Full name _____
(BLOCK CAPITALS)
In the event of my death, if possible contact:

    Tel. _____

Name _____

In the hope that I might help others, I hereby make this gift, to take effect upon my death. The words and marks below indicate my commitment.

For purposes of transplantation, medical education, or research, I give—

_____ any needed organs and tissues.

_____ only the following organs and tissues:

American Red Cross ✚

Do you carry a kidney donor card like the ones shown in the picture?
How many people in your class carry donor cards?
If you don't carry a donor card, what are your reasons for not doing so?
If you do carry a donor card, why did you decide to do so?
Are you worried that a mistake might be made if you are unconscious rather than dead after an accident, for example?

2 Episode 1 – emergency

There is a young child in the renal unit of a district hospital (a unit for patients with kidney problems). She is connected to a dialysis machine because her kidneys are not functioning. She desperately needs a kidney transplant.

There is no one in her family who can help. Doctors think that they will get a kidney for her soon and she is first on the hospital waiting list. She will not survive much longer without a new kidney.

Suddenly, one of the country's leading medical scientists is rushed into the unit. He is on the verge of discovering a cure for arthritis, but has suffered acute kidney failure. Doctors quickly discover that he is in very bad shape. There are no other dialysis machines. He has only two days to live unless he gets a transplant.

Miraculously, a kidney is found. The doctors have to decide who to operate on.

What is your advice to them? With a few other students, consider the choices and reasons. Decide on your advice to the doctors, then compare your decision with another group or with the class.

3 Episode 2 – an angry nurse

The doctors decide to operate on the scientist. One of the nurses who cares for the young child is angered by the decision. She believes that the waiting list is the only fair way of deciding transplants. She is wondering whether to inform the press.

If the press hear of the doctors' decision, the hospital will receive damaging publicity and kidney sufferers will get nervous. But should doctors be allowed to ignore the waiting list?

What would you advise the nurse to do and why? Talk about this issue with your group, decide on the right advice to give, then see whether others agree with your ideas.

4 Episode 3 – black market

Although it is not common knowledge, the kidney used in the operation was bought illegally on the black market. The surgeon arranged all this but the scientist's family paid for the kidney.

The surgeon who performed the operation is now feeling a growing sense of guilt. Should she confess this information, lose her job and raise doubts about the donor's kidney, or should she just keep quiet? After all, a life has been saved and a cure for arthritis will now be quickly available.

Share your thoughts on this moral dilemma with your group.

5 The final episode – what happens?

Can you offer a credible conclusion to this tale?
In your group, discuss some possibilities. For example:

– The medical scientist recovers but the child dies.
– Another kidney is found quickly and the child recovers.
– The story is discovered by a reporter and publicised. There are questions asked in the national press about the whole donor programme, and the shortage of kidneys becomes an even more serious problem. The surgeon is put on trial.
– The medical scientist suddenly becomes ill again with a serious blood disorder. The scientist's family are convinced that the transplanted kidney is a diseased one and want to publicise the whole event in an effort to locate another kidney quickly. The surgeon tries to stop them.
– The medical scientist becomes ill again. His family pay for another kidney, but he dies before he can receive it.

Talk about a likely outcome, then tell it to the class.

6 A twist of fate

The episodes you have been considering are based upon a real story. Listen to the outcome on the cassette.

12 | Winner takes all

Gambling

1 Two up

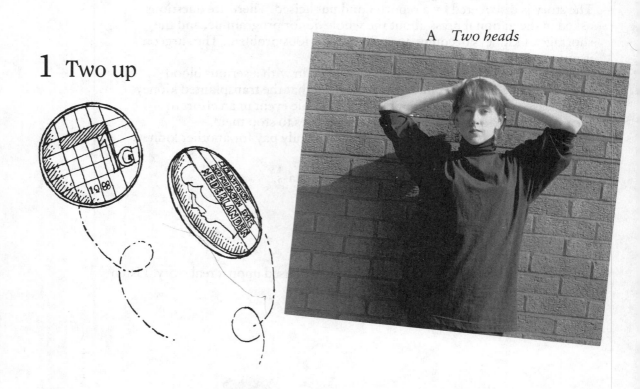

A   *Two heads*

Play this simple game that is often played in Australia for fun. The teacher is going to throw two coins up and let them fall.
Stand in a circle and show how you think they are going to fall:

Two heads – put both hands on your head (A)
One head and one tail – one hand on head, one hand on back (B)
Two tails – both hands on back (C)

If you were wrong, leave the circle. If you were right, stay in and play a second time. The winner is the last person to remain in the circle.

Talk about your experience of the game. Did you find it interesting?
How many throws did your class need to find a winner?
In what ways could the game be played for money?
Do you think it would be more interesting if played for money?

B   *A head and a tail*

C   *Two tails*

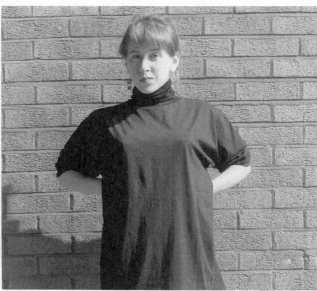

2 Attitudes to gambling

Does gambling, in either public or private form, exist in your country?

If your answer is 'yes', talk about these questions with one or two other students:

> What are the most popular types of gambling in your country?
> Are there dangers or disadvantages associated with gambling?
> Does your government raise money by having a national lottery?
> Is this a good idea?

If your answer is 'no', talk about these questions with one or two other students:

> What are the reasons for not having gambling in your country?
> Are there people who would like to gamble?
> Is it important for the law to prevent gambling?
> Would you be in favour of a national form of gambling, like a lottery, to raise money for helping people?

If you are all from the same country, can you agree on your answers?
If you are not all from the same country, compare your own answers and ideas with those of someone from a different country.

3 I had a little flutter . . .

Have any of you ever placed bets on:

   a card game?   horses?   boats?   a game with dice?
   other .... ?

If you have, tell the others about your experiences. Are you naturally lucky,
or naturally unlucky?

4 I'm the world's worst gambler . . .

Listen to these people talking about their experience of gambling. As you
listen, write down the type of gambling they mention and try to remember
one of their stories.

	Type of gambling	What happened?
Speaker 1	Poker	play all night / Spain 65 quid
Speaker 2	boat race	20:1 won 10 dollars
Speaker 3	Casino	stand next to people who wins

(handwritten notes: she won (pounds) a full house / Sydney Harbour / Monte Carlo / had a flutter + lost)

Check your answers with other students. In groups of three, take it in turns
to retell the stories. Help each other to remember as many details as possible.

5 Could you be a successful gambler?

Look at these situations. Tick one of the two choices.

1 You have to pay your rent tomorrow: $200. You have $5, so you:
   a) put the $5 on a horse.
   b) try to borrow money from a friend.   2

2 You are studying for an examination. You:
   a) read all your lecture notes several times.   0
   b) guess what is going to be in the exam and study that only.

3 A friend asks you to buy a raffle ticket. The money will help the local school. You:
   a) buy one ticket to help the school.   1
   b) buy ten to have a better chance of winning a prize.

4 You are going to a new place for a holiday. You:
   a) don't arrange anything in advance, just hope for the best.   0
   b) arrange everything before you leave home.

5 You buy an expensive watch in another country. Coming home, you:
   a) wear it and walk confidently through customs.   8
   b) declare it, to be on the safe side.

6 You are going abroad for a weekend only. You:
   a) insure yourself just in case.   0
   b) do not take out insurance and hope nothing happens.

7 You notice that your boss has made a mistake. You:
   a) tell her or him politely.   3
   b) smile sweetly and remain silent.

8 You meet a stranger on a plane, who asks you out for a drink. You:
   a) accept.   b) refuse politely.   2

9 You are looking for a new house or flat. A friend rings up and says he has seen the ideal one, but you have to decide instantly. You:
   a) refuse — you can't buy anything without seeing it.   0
   b) take a chance on it.

10 You are taking part in a political rally. The police arrive and tell everyone to go home. You:
   a) sit down and hope you will not be arrested.   3
   b) go quietly.   19

Look at the key and count up your score.

Sit in small groups and try to guess one another's scores and profiles.
Are any of you 'born gamblers'?

13 | A roll of the dice

Making risky decisions

1 Shall I stay or shall I go?

In small groups, discuss the events that are shown in this picture. Can you imagine what happened? Try to build a story that is as complete as possible.

Listen to the cassette and with a few others, talk about the decision that you have to make.

2 In or out?

You can now take part in a game of chance. If you choose to be involved, you will roll the dice to get a number. You must then accept the instructions which go with your number.
If you do not wish to take part, you can be an observer of the activity, and report back to the class.

Decide: Are you going to be in the game of chance or out?

3 Rolling the dice

Players: Go to the front of the class and roll the dice to get your number. Form a group with everyone who got the same number as you. Your teacher will give the group your instructions.

Observers: Join one of the groups as an observer.

4 Following the instructions

Players: In your group, discuss the instructions. Make a list of your biggest worries about what you have to do.

Observers: Listen to what people say and observe their reactions.

5 Odds and evens

Players: Join with other groups – odd numbers together (1,3,5) and even numbers together (2,4,6).
Tell the others about your instructions and your worries about them.
Decide which of the instructions was the most favourable, and which was the least favourable.

Observers: Join together and share your observations of the various groups. Give your own reactions to the activity. Are you glad you did not join in? Prepare a short report on the whole game of chance for the class.

6 Reporting back

Observers: Give your report to the whole class. Describe what you observed and your own opinions of the game of chance.

Players: What were your reactions to the game of chance? Do you agree with the observers' views?

⬛ As a class, consider all instructions. Listen to all six on the cassette if you like. Which one do you consider the most difficult? Why?
Are there any of the instructions that you could realistically follow? Give your reasons.

14 | What's on tonight?
TV, films, video

1 Stargazing

1
2
3
4
5
6

In groups of three, see if you can name these famous film stars and identify which country they come from. You score one point for every correct answer. The maximum possible score is 12.

What is your group's score? You now have five minutes to interview other groups. Can you add to your score?

In your groups, talk about the film or television stars you know. Do any of you have favourites? Explain why you like these stars particularly.

2 Movie talk

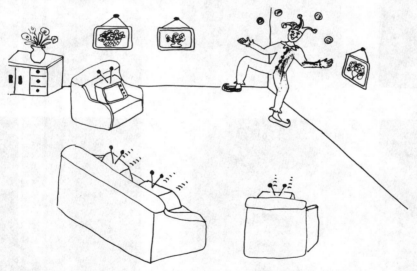

Listen to two people talking about their favourite film. Write down the name of the film, and make a few notes about what each person says.

	name of the film	*details of the film*
Film 1		
Film 2		

Compare names and notes with one or two other students.

Now, write the name of one of your favourite films on a piece of paper. Exchange papers with another student. Ask your partner questions about the film. Are there two people in the class with the same favourite film?

3 TV questionnaire

Answer the questions opposite, then in pairs, compare your answers and scores.

What do you think a high score (25–30) or a low score (0–6) means? Write a description of people with those scores. Try to add another question to the questionnaire.
Join another pair and compare your 'profiles' and your new questions. Can you agree on what the scores mean?

Do you think you are too dependent on TV for entertainment and information? Discuss this question together.

Answer the following questions:

1   **Friends arrive unexpectedly, just at the most exciting part of a film you are watching on TV. Do you:**
    a)   switch off the TV immediately?
    b)   try to persuade the friends to watch the TV for a while?
    c)   talk to them and watch the TV at the same time?

2   **You have arrived home from work tired after a hard day's work. Do you:**
    a)   flop down in a chair and watch the TV for the evening?
    b)   go to bed early with a good book?
    c)   watch a bit of TV, then listen to some restful music for the evening?

3   **On average how much television do you watch each week?**
    a)   None at all.
    b)   1—10 hours.
    c)   10—20 hours.

4   **Your children (or some children who are staying with you) ask you if they can get up at six a.m. to watch cartoons on TV. Do you:**
    a)   say 'yes' but tell them not to wake you?
    b)   say 'no' immediately?
    c)   tell them they can watch the cartoons on this occasion only?

5   **With which of these statements do you agree most?**
    a)   Television has severely damaged the art of good conversation.
    b)   Television is a great source of information and entertainment.
    c)   Television is OK when you are tired and alone.

6   **Do you:**
    a)   enjoy talking about all sorts of TV programmes you have seen the day after watching them?
    b)   occasionally talk about TV programmes when they are exceptionally good or interesting?
    c)   never talk about TV programmes?

Scores: 1 a) 0   b) 5   c) 3   4 a) 5   b) 0   c) 3
              2 a) 5   b) 0   c) 3   5 a) 3   b) 5   c) 0
              3 a) 0   b) 3   c) 5   6 a) 5   b) 3   c) 0

4 To the lighthouse

Imagine that you have to spend one week by yourself, looking after a lighthouse.
You can take with you three books or three videos. Make a list of the three.
Ask other people in the class about their lists, and tell them about the books or videos on your list.
In the class as a whole, were more books or more videos chosen?

5 What's on in town?

As a class, go to see a film in your town, or watch one on TV or video. Work with a partner. Each pair chooses one of the tasks from the box. Talk about it in class so that different people are doing different tasks.

Talk about your favourite scenes.
Talk about the performance of one of the main actors in the film.
Talk about the story: what was most interesting about it?
Talk about . . . (Add your own suggestion.)

Next class: Each pair prepares a report together, then presents it to the class. If you like, you can also display written reports and visuals of the film.

15 | Soaps
Writing a popular TV show

1 What do you think about soaps?

Soaps are TV dramas about ordinary people and their lives. They are shown regularly, and are like continuing plays.

Interview two other students in the class about soaps:
— If they have a favourite soap, ask about the main characters and situations.
— If they never watch soaps, ask if they have heard of any and what they think of soaps generally.

Feedback: What soaps do people in your class watch? What about your teacher?

2 Sky ways: planning a new soap

Form a group of three students. You are script writers. You have been hired by a TV company to plan a new soap for their TV channel, a soap about people working for an international airline. This new show must be popular and win a lot of viewers.

Decide upon some exciting situations for one of the episodes. You will need dramatic events to make viewers interested and help them to identify with the main characters.

Here are some possible ideas. Use these or your own:
— a hijack in which one hijacker is related to one of the crew
— part of the aircraft drops off in mid-flight
— a love affair between a pilot and a flight attendant
— the airline's first woman flight captain
— a crew member disappears in a distant country in between flights
— the pilot's wife wants her husband to change his job because he is away from home so much
— others ....

Together, write a rough outline of your events.

3 Casting the characters

Make a list of the characters in your soap. Create first and family names for them.
Possible roles include: pilots, first officers, navigators, flight attendants, engineers, hijackers, managing director, wives, husbands of key characters.

Study the faces of these actors. Together, choose the ones that seem suitable for your roles.
Compare your characters and names with those of other groups.

4 Developing the characters

In your groups, choose two different characters. Discuss their personalities and start to build up descriptions of each of them, using these headings:

– personality   (kind, bad-tempered, easy going, humorous, etc.)
– background   (poor/rich family, brilliant/average intelligence, strict father / exotic mother / jealous brother, etc.)
– 'skeleton in the cupboard'   (e.g. once killed someone in a driving accident; schizophrenic grandfather; recent history of blackouts, etc.)
– hobbies/beliefs/attitudes   (likes fishing; worries about threats to airline safety from increased numbers of flights; believes they'll die in a crash one day)

When you are ready, join another group and tell them about your two characters.

5 Writing the draft of a scene

Option A

In your groups, write some dialogue for the scene you outlined in your first planning session. Before you write, talk about the scene and about the characters involved.

Option B

If you prefer, you can use this story board of three pictures for your episode. In it, the pilot's window blows out unexpectedly and he is nearly sucked out of the aircraft.

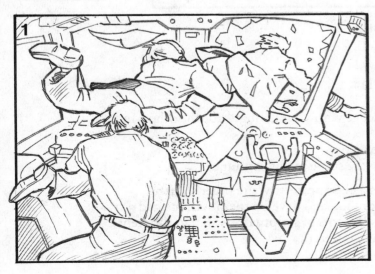

6 Performing the scene

Introduce and then perform your scene with your dialogue for the others in
the class. Ask for comments.

Was the dialogue exciting, clear, realistic?

What ideas can others give for how the scene might continue?

If you like, you can continue this as a class project. Write other short
episodes or scenes for your airline drama, and develop the situations and
lives of the characters. Work in small teams of scriptwriters so that different
teams develop their own situations in different ways.

16 | Have you got Mexican red-knees?

Pets and other animals

1 A cuddly stick insect

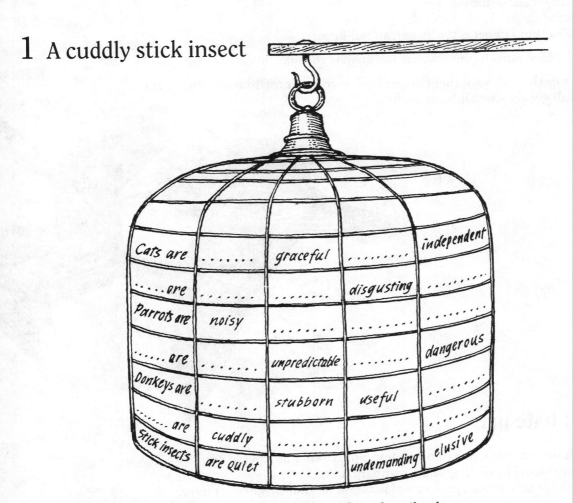

Cats are	....	graceful	....	independent
.... are	....	....	disgusting	....
Parrots are	noisy	....	....	....
.... are	....	unpredictable	....	dangerous
Donkeys are	....	stubborn	useful	....
.... are	cuddly	....	....	....
Stick insects	are quiet	....	undemanding	elusive

With a partner, fill in the pet column, then add words to describe the pets.
See if you can fill in all the spaces, but try not to use the same word twice.
If you have any problems, ask another pair – will they give you a word in
exchange for one of yours?

As a class, list all the pets you have named. Which are the three most popular
pets in your country?

2 She's an absolute pet!

What is a 'Mexican red-knee'? Does anyone in your class know? If you don't know, can you guess?

You are going to listen to a woman talking about her pets. But first, look at these questions below with another student.

— Which pets does the woman keep?
— Can you describe Annie?
— What do red-knees eat?
— What kind of pet is the 'Mexican red-knee'?

Now listen to the woman and answer the questions.

Get together with another pair and ask each other the four questions. Have you all got the same information?

3 I hate pets!

What do you think of having a Mexican red-knee as a pet in your dining-room? In small groups, compare reactions.
Tell the others about any unusual pets you or your neighbours have.

People keep pets for many reasons. Can you add to the lists?
— to keep them company   — as a hobby
— ....   — ....
— ....   — ....

Some people hate pets. See if there are any pet haters in your class. Ask them why. Can you use any of the reasons to persuade them to change their mind?

4 Amazing birds

These birds may look quite ordinary but they are amazing. Can you guess
why? Talk about possible reasons with another student.
Together, try to complete these sentences:

The white-throated needle tail is believed to fly from breeding grounds in
northern Asia to Tasmania and back again without ....
....

The red-necked stint weighs little more than a box of matches but flies the
farthest of any shore bird, an incredible .... kilometres round trip
from Siberia to Tasmania.

The arctic tern travels .... kilometres on the longest migratory
journey of any bird on earth.

Compare your answers.

5 A sense of direction

What would be your answers to these other questions about bird migration?
– How do birds survive such long journeys?
– How do birds find their way to their destinations when they migrate?
– Why do birds migrate?
– Do migrating birds travel mainly by day or at night?
Discuss your theories with one or two other students. Perhaps a good encyclopedia will help you with some answers.

Some scientists believe that birds have an in-built compass that enables them to navigate. Do you have an in-built compass that helps you when you are looking for a certain place, or when you are lost? With one or two other students, talk about differences in your sense of direction. Are some people in your class 'geographically blind' – that is, they have no sense of direction at all?

17 | A man's best friend?
Dangerous dogs

1 Frightening attacks

In many towns and cities in the world, people are worried about large dogs attacking children in the streets or in their homes. In one case, three dogs went into a primary school playground and attacked several children.
Is this a worry in your country?
Have you heard of similar attacks? Talk about this problem with one or two others.

2 On the line

Imagine that the wall of your classroom is a line going from opinion A
(No one should be allowed to keep dangerous pets in towns), to opinion B
(Careful owners have a right to keep pets of any kind).

Go and stand somewhere along the wall. Your position will show your
opinion.

3 Stop Dangerous Dogs and Friends of the Dog

Form groups of three or four with other students standing near you. Use task
sheet A if you are closer to opinion A; use task sheet B if you are closer to
opinion B.

Task sheet A

Your group is called SDD (Stop Dangerous Dogs). You have received a lot of information about dangerous pets. Read the following article:

Dog snatches baby from sitting-room

'I only popped out to the kitchen', sobbed Mrs. Brenda Olivares, as she remembered the horrific moment.

'I left the front door open, it was a hot day. Sara was in her little cradle in the front room.

When I got back there was this great big dog. He was pulling her from the cradle and holding on to her shoulder with his teeth. It was horrifying'.

Other similar examples in the last two years:
— Two boys were attacked in Sweden when they gave sweets to a neighbour's dog.
— A postman in Ireland lost the end of his finger as he pushed letters into a letter box.
— A young girl was badly bitten by the family pet (a Dobermann). The dog had always been friendly before that.

A U.S. study of owners of dangerous pets shows that:
— Young people are using large dogs as fashion accessories.
— Owners of dangerous dogs are people who are afraid of violence in modern towns
— Owners of aggressive dogs are psychologically weak – they use dogs to do their fighting for them.

Your task:
Consider the information you have received. Think about these questions:

Do individual people have the right to own dogs that may become dangerous?
What laws are needed to prevent horrific attacks on children by dogs?
What should be done with people who do not obey the laws? Should their pets be killed?
Should dog owners pay a special tax?

As a group decide on at least two new recommendations to present to an International Conference on Human Safety.

Task sheet B

Your group is called FOD (Friends of the Dog). You know that people are getting worried about dangerous dogs. However, you have received a lot of information about dogs that have protected their owners from personal attack or burglary. Read the following:

Baby saved by dog

'. . . I was just standing looking in a shop window in the town centre when I heard this terrible noise', said Mrs Sondheim.

'There was this dog barking its head off, and I saw this woman lifting a little baby from a pram . . . and the dog got hold of her coat and kept shaking it and growling, and just wouldn't let go.

Finally the woman put the baby back and the dog let go and she ran off.'

Other examples include:
– A pet dog discovered a bag of dangerous drugs hidden in the garage next to an old factory.
– Thieves broke into the home of 80-year-old Mary Schwartz twice in one year. Then she bought a large dog (Rottweiler) for protection. She hasn't had any problems since then.
– A student was taking his dog for a walk in a city park when someone came up to him with a knife. The dog ran out of the bushes towards the attacker who dropped the knife and ran off.

Studies show that:
– Older people are more worried than they used to be about violence. They are happier when they can have a large dog to protect them.
– Research results show that people with pets are less likely to suffer from loneliness or depression.
– People say that you need protection and having a dog is more acceptable than having a gun.

Your task:
Consider the information you have received. Think about these questions:

How can we make sure that the public knows that most dogs are friendly?
How can we detect and deal with dog owners who do not control their dogs?
How can we save our individual right to have a dog as a companion and for protection? The newspapers are exaggerating the problem of dangerous dogs.

As a group decide on at least two recommendations to take to the International Conference on Human Safety.

4 The International Conference on Human Safety

Form groups of six or eight with equal numbers from SDD and FOD.
Each side: Present your recommendations. Give reasons for your decisions.

Discuss the recommendations. Choose the most important ones – at least
two – that everyone can agree upon.

5 Feedback

As a class, share the ideas that came from the groups. Did all the groups have
similar opinions?
Are the recommendations suitable for the situation in your own country?
Give reasons why or why not.
If you stood on the line between opinion A and opinion B again, would you
take the same position?

18 Good fences make good neighbours

Neighbours and neighbouring countries

1 An ideal neighbour

What makes a good neighbour?
Put a tick in the appropriate boxes, add other things if you wish, then
compare with your neighbour in the classroom.
Discuss differences of opinion.

My ideal neighbour would be:	*Yes*	*No*
a family with children	☐	☐
a single professional person	☐	☐
people who share my interests	☐	☐
people who often come over for a chat	☐	☐
people I never see	☐	☐
someone without pets	☐	☐
a very quiet person	☐	☐
a party-loving person	☐	☐
....	☐	☐
....	☐	☐

2 Good neighbours, bad neighbours and strange neighbours

ordinary   calm   jolly   quiet   reserved
shy   polite   helpful   neighbourly   friendly
kind   warmhearted   gentle   sociable
hospitable
generous   understanding   strange
co-operative   cheerful   bizarre
honest

noisy   quarrelsome   nosy   unkind
rowdy   busybody   hostile   rude
vicious   inhospitable
bad-tempered   unfriendly   petty
unsociable   cruel
unhelpful   deceitful   unwilling

Think about the best, the worst, or the strangest neighbour you ever had. Tick any words above which describe that neighbour. If there are words you don't know, ask other students or look in the dictionary.

Sit with two other students. Tell each other about the neighbour – why did you tick the words you did?

3 It was such a nice neighbourhood!

Listen to the two speakers talking about the way their neighbourhoods have changed over the years.
With another student, fill in as many details as you can in the following grid:

	changes for the better	*changes for the worse*
Speaker 1		
Speaker 2		

Compare your details with those of another pair.
What about your own neighbourhood? Have you noticed changes in it since you began living in it? Talk about the changes you have seen – or would like to see – with other students.

4 Neighbouring countries

If countries could be moved, this is how the authors would put them. In
small groups, discuss the changes that are on this map.
Do you think the new neighbours would get along well?
Can you imagine any problems that might arise?

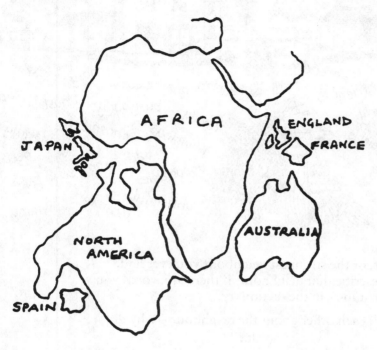

5 Ideal neighbours

If you could draw a new map of the world, which countries in the world
would you choose as neighbours?

With another student, choose at least two countries for your new
neighbours. Draw a rough map, then join another pair. Show your map and
explain it to each other.
Have you chosen different or similar neighbours?

19 | Boundary disputes
Quarrels with neighbours

1 We shall live in peace for the next ten years

Sit in groups of four. Imagine that you are four good friends. You've been living in flats in a large city and you decide to move to the country, buy a house and live together.

In your groups, imagine the situation. Talk about how you would feel. What kind of house and garden would you like? How would you spend your free time? Can you all agree?

2 The answerphone message

Now imagine that the four of you have been in the house one month. You feel quite happy there. You have started planting trees in your garden and growing vegetables.
One day, you come in to find a message on your answerphone.

🔲 Listen to the message.

Together, decide how to react to the message:
— Will you speak to the neighbour directly? (Together, decide what you will say to him.)
— Will you go and see your lawyer? (Together, decide what you will ask him.)
— Will you quickly put up a fence round the whole garden, because you are sure it belongs to you? (Together, discuss what will happen: how will the neighbour react?)
— Or will you do something else? ....
....

(Discuss what will happen as a result.)

Make a note of what you decide to do.

3 Prompt action

The very next morning, before you have had time to do anything, one of your group goes out in the car and notices that the neighbour has already taken some action. She stops to have a closer look. What do you think the neighbour has done?

🔲 There is a telephone nearby so she phones the rest of you who are in the house to tell you the news.

Together, decide how you will react.
Are you going to:

— Do nothing and let the neighbour get away with it? (What will happen?)
— Try to speak with the neighbour? (What will you say to him?)
— Take revenge and do something horrible in return? (What? Cut down some of his trees? Feed poison to his dog? Put your cassette player as close to his house as possible and play loud music night and day?)
— Talk to the police or a lawyer about the situation? (This could take a long time and be expensive.)
— Other ideas? ....
....

Make a note of what you plan to do and why.

4 Never decide in haste or in anger   (optional activity)

After you have planned what you are going to do, you decide to tell some friends about your problem. Your friends are reasonable people who can give you advice and tell you if your plan is a good one or not.

Form new groups. Two of you join up with two from another group. Take it in turns to present your plan. When the two others are describing their plan, play the role of the friends. Listen to what they say.

Discuss these questions:
— Will the plan stop the problem?
— Will it be too expensive?
— Will it cause a lot of hatred?
— Will it let the neighbours be friends?

Discuss each plan in turn. Is it a good plan? Can you suggest a better idea?

5 Is revenge sweet?

If you did Activity 4, move back into your original groups. Now imagine that as you walk back to your house after speaking with your friends, you see your neighbour stuck in a tree. His hand is bleeding and his ladder has fallen to the ground.
You can choose to help or not. Decide together what you are going to do.

6 Feedback

As a class, talk about what people decided to do in the situation. Did most people react in the same way? Can you all agree on the best thing to do? Have any of you ever been involved in a problem of this kind with people you live near to? What happened?

Perhaps some of you live in flats and often have to put bicycles or prams in shared areas. Does this cause a problem? What about noise, shared stairways, bathrooms?

20 | Memorials

*Remembering and
commemorating*

1 Forget me not

These pictures show
ways of remembering
people or animals.
With another student, try
to think of three more
places where you might
see memorials of this
kind. Share your ideas
with another group.

2 They were just getting to the most difficult part . . .

Listen to people telling stories which are possible explanations for three of
the memorials in the pictures. Match each story with the appropriate
memorial.

	Memorial
Story 1	
Story 2	
Story 3	

The three speakers do not finish their stories. Choose one of the stories and
discuss possible endings with two other students.
Find two other students who chose different stories. Tell each other the
whole stories with your endings.

3 Visiting the Peace Gardens in Hiroshima

Study the map and the picture and then
try to answer these three questions:

1 What is the name of the building?
   a) Hiroshima castle
   b) Peace cathedral
   c) Atom Bomb Dome

2 In what year did the atomic bomb explode on Hiroshima?
   a) 1947
   b) 1945
   c) 1949

3 Approximately how many people were killed?
   a) 200,000
   b) 35,000
   c) 75,000

Listen to a guide taking tourists round the Peace Gardens in
Hiroshima. Were your answers to the three questions correct? What other
details can you give about the Peace Gardens?

Would you like to visit the Peace Gardens? If you have done so, talk about
the experience to your class. What did you find most unforgettable?

4 In our town, there is . . .

Homework: With a partner if possible, look around your town or the town you are living in. Make notes about statues, fine old buildings, or places that commemorate someone or something.
Write a short list, using a few words to describe what the buildings or other places look like.
You can use these words if you like. Ask another student to help you with words you don't know, or look in a dictionary.

unusual?
drab?
impressive?
neglected?
striking?
hideous?
attractive?
grotesque?
moving?

Next class, in small groups, compare lists and talk about the memorials, using some of the words you chose. Give as many details as you can about the things or people that are commemorated.

5 Ladies and gentlemen, we are standing in front of . . .

With a partner, choose a memorial or another interesting place or building in your town. Imagine that you are a tourist guide. Prepare a short talk to tell tourists about it. Discuss with your partner ways of making the talk as interesting as possible.
Try your talk out on each other.

When you are ready, change partners. Each is a guide and gives the short talk.
Listeners: Tell your partner the most interesting thing about the talk you heard.
Some of you might like to give your talk to the class.

6 Memorial to this book

Write an epitaph to this book and send it to the authors. You can choose one of these, but better still, make up your own.

Key

Unit 1   1.1 The present in the photo is a tennis racket.   1.3 Information to be given to B and C: After receiving the tickets, B meets a new friend and instantly falls in love. B decides not to go to Nairobi after all.

Unit 2   2.3
1 Fat people are jollier than thin people.
2 Teachers are kinder to good-looking pupils.
3 People who wear a lot of jewellery or perfume tend to be frivolous.
4 Intelligent people are usually plain.
5 Short people are more aggressive than tall people.
6 Untidy people are often lazy.
7 It's hard to trust very beautiful people.

Unit 3   3.1 The pieces of dance music on the cassette are, in this order: Russian (B); Bolivian (C); Scottish (A); Indian (D).

Unit 5   5.1 Speaker 1:3; Speaker 2:4; Speaker 3:5; Speaker 4:2.   5.3 (colours of precious stones) ruby – red; sapphire – blue; emerald – green; topaz – reddish yellow; amethyst – purple; diamond – transparent.

Birthstones:

January – garnet	July – ruby
February – amethyst	August – sardonyx
March – aquamarine	September – sapphire
April – diamond	October – opal
May – emerald	November – topaz
June – pearl	December – turquoise

Unit 10   10.2 Type of exercise and number of calories burned per minute: badminton: 10; climbing: 12; cycling: 5–12 (depends on speed); dancing: 5–7; gymnastics: 6; jogging: 10; long distance running: 11; tennis: 7; swimming: 11–14; golf: 5.   10.3 The sport is called bungy jumping.   10.4 Possible answers: backwards, run, prevent, bicycle, laugh.

Unit 11   11.1 1) bigger   2) 24 hours   3) right

pelvis   4) 1½ hours approximately if the operation has no complications   5) to clear blood of waste products

Unit 12   12.5 Scores:
1a–10, 1b–2;   2a–0, 2b–5;
3a–1, 3b–5;   4a–7, 4b–0;
5a–8, 5b–1;   6a–6, 6b–0;
7a–3, 7b–7;   8a–8, 8b–2;
9a–0, 9b–9;   10a–7, 10b–3.
Profile: 10–25: You are not a natural born gambler, but a little flutter now and then wouldn't do any harm.
25–40: You could be a moderately successful gambler, but do not seem to be in danger of becoming an addict.
40–60: You like a taste of danger! Be careful, you might become addicted!
60–75: You are definitely a born gambler. Have you thought of joining Gamblers Anonymous?

Unit 13   13.1 The painting by Robert Dodd (1790) shows a famous nineteenth-century mutiny when some of the crew members of English ship The Bounty rebelled against their harsh captain and set him adrift in the Pacific Ocean.   13.3 Instructions to give to groups that have rolled the following numbers:
1 You must prepare for a journey of self discovery. You must leave friends and loved ones within 30 days and journey to a far land. You must enter the lives of three people in that land and help them to survive and live a fruitful life.
2 You must exchange lives with another person in your class. For a period of three months you will live his or her life and he or she will live your life. The exchange must be complete.
3 You must give up life as you now know it and join the tramps and vagrants in the city. You must participate fully in their lives and use the wisdom that you gain in your own life. You must live as a street dweller for one year.
4 You must first fly in balloons, gliders, and hang gliders. Feel like a bird, free in the air. From this freedom in the skies you must learn the value of space and spend three months alone in a dark underground cave with only candles, books, food and drink. This is your chance to test your strength of character and to conquer loneliness.

5 You must go to live among wild animals. Study them, learn their ways, live as they do. You must not speak your own language or read or listen to it for a period of six months but you can imitate the call of the animals.

6 You will receive a large amount of money. You must spend it all on yourself during a period of two months. Even if you are tempted to give things to others, you must resist. Indulge yourself in all those ways you have dreamt of but never thought possible, but do so alone. You must not share your fortune with anyone.

Unit 14 **14.1** 1 Liv Ullman, Norway 2 Whoopi Goldberg, USA 3 Buster Keaton, USA 4 Shashi Kapoor, India 5 Bruce Lee, born USA, Chinese parents 6 Meryl Streep, USA

Unit 16 **16.2** The Mexican red-knee is a breed of spider. **16.4** 1) without touching the ground; 2) 24,000 km; 3) 40,000 km.

Unit 20 **20.3** 1 (c) 2 (b) 3 (a) but estimates vary.

Tapescript

Unit 1   A dozen red potatoes

2   Tickets and pictures
A: Well, the most memorable present I've ever had was . . . a dozen red potatoes . . . (*laughs*) It makes me feel very warm, just thinking about them, red potatoes . . .
B: And full . . .
A: And full. (*laughs*) Um, I was going out with a really, really lovely . . . man, and the only thing that . . . that spoilt our relationship was that he was a . . . a great meat eater, and, on Valentine's Day he invited me to his home . . . and said he'd cook me a meal . . . and I was a bit worried about this, I didn't know what he was going to do. And when I got there he had the table set beautifully with candles and silver and . . . a big silver platter on my plate, with a cover. And I sat down and he removed this cover from the silver platter and there were a dozen red potatoes.
B: Did you have . . . did you have to eat them then and there?

A: No . . . he made a beautiful vegetarian dish for me . . . and it's not been a problem since.
B: Very good.
C: The worst present . . . I ever had is one that's still with us, in fact. My wife's sister, um . . . she fancies herself as a bit of an artist. And ah . . . she's also particularly fond of purple. And . . . ah, we moved into a new house . . . uh . . . just outside London and as a housewarming gift my wife's sister decided to paint us a very large purple abstract painting. (*laughter*) And she said, ah . . . as she gave it . . . gave us this gift, with . . . um, with a great deal of glee, she said, 'I thought it would be absolutely perfect above the fireplace.' (*laughter*) Unfortunately, she comes to visit us quite a lot . . .
B: Oh, no . . .
C: And, uh . . . we hung it over the fireplace . . . uh . . . (*laughter*) . . . but we do take it down and we put it back up (*laughter*) when we know she's coming. (*laughter*)
D: The best Christmas present I ever had was from my boyfriend at the time, who was actually working in Kenya. And . . . he rang me on the morning of the second of December, and said what would I like for Christmas, 'cause he thought he'd better post it then. And I really didn't know, I hadn't put my mind to Christmas, so I said, you know, I . . . I don't mind, I . . . I'll leave, leave it to your . . . discretion. And about ten days later in the post, um . . . there was a recorded delivery in fact, which I had to sign for, and inside was a return flight to Nairobi . . .

4   Quack, quack . . . quack, quack . . .
Can you answer that, please?
(*laughs*) Well, first of all I have to laugh. (*laughs*) That's my first impression, is that I have to laugh. Looking at it, there's a lot of expertise that has gone into it . . . ah . . . but I'm not too certain whether I'm sold by the idea. I much prefer to give this duck to one of my children to put into a bath. (*laughter*) Anyway . . . but I like the idea of a phone being made out of a duck ornament. But . . . ah . . . it's a bit expensive for me.

I think it's quite amusing but also rather silly,

considering what it is. Um . . . yes, too expensive to give to children . . . um . . . I can't imagine actually using it and giving bad news or receiving bad news on it, I'd, I'd feel rather stupid. Um . . . no. Give me a Mickey Mouse phone any day. (*laughter*)

Yeah, I, I can't help but agree. I . . . I hardly know where to begin, really. Um . . . it just seems like a, a waste of time . . . and the eyes lighting up, that's the final touch . . . it quacks, and then you pick the head off of it, (*laughter*) and eyes light up. I just . . . it would, it would . . . scare me. Can you imagine coming down into a darkened room, and . . . ah, the eyes are lighting up of this duck and it's quacking? No, no, no, no, sorry . . .

Unit 3 Rhythm and blues

1 Dances of the world
(Extracts of dance music from the following countries: Russia, Bolivia, Scotland, India.)

2 The last time I went dancing . . .
When I came to London, what I enjoyed most was doing classical dance, because it was so different from Nigerian dancing. Why? Because you could hold on to a bar and do all these sorts of positions: there was one, two, three, four and five. I enjoyed fifth position because I had a very good 'turn out'. That is what they called it: turn out. It meant that your feet could go out like little fish feet. Yes, I enjoyed it very much. But I didn't like the teacher. He was always shouting and because I came from Nigeria he thought I didn't understand him. But I'd been speaking English from the age of one or two.

The last time I went dancing, I went to a town hall for a New Year's Eve celebration. It was a very unusual New Year's Eve because it was um . . . it was a Persian New Year's Eve. Then they started to dance. And it was a kind of belly dance. And as a small child I had got smacked soundly for doing the belly dance. And I found when I got up to do this dance, um . . . I felt very shy and very soon I had to sit down, and I could not get up again to dance. I felt just like a little girl again.

3 My feet just start tapping . . .
(Four pieces of dance music: Disco, Egyptian belly dancing, Flamenco, African.)

4 Morris dancing
(Morris dancing music)

A: So you're a Morris dancer!

B: Well I'm not a Morris dancer but I have done Morris dancing, um, . . . it's a hobby and it's been traditional, you know, in this country, for hundreds and hundreds of years. Um, you know they have ribbons that are tied on their arms and their legs (*ah huh*) and bells which are usually tied round the knees . . . and handbells as well.

A: And . . . the handkerchiefs or something . . .

B: And the handkerchiefs, yeah, they, they wave handkerchiefs, and there's also a hobby horse and er, there's a man called the Fool who is sort of the leader of the troupe, who is the sort of, (*ah huh*) the funny one. Usually they're not very funny at all but . . . (*laughter*) who, who goes round waving a, a . . . the bladder. Er, all these things, um, er, you know have been, they're, they're they've been around for, for years and years and years. And they have sticks as well . . . um . . . which they knock against each other. (*ah huh*), Ah, and er, people think, think that it's evolved from sword dances, er, and the sticks were, replaced er . . . swords. And in fact in some parts of England they still use swords. Um, and it was always a dance that was done in springtime . . . um.

A: But they do it all, they do it all the time now . . .

B: Oh they do it, yes . . .

A: What about the hobby horse? That, they had like a, you know, a horse (*that's right*) that they . . . Dancing and stuff . . . (*Well*) does that mean anything?

B: Well, it's, it's it's again a traditional sort of mediaeval ritual. Um, in spring or sometimes at the harvest you'd get a man disguised as a horse, wearing a horse's skull and he'd go round knocking on people's doors with . . . and he'd be accompanied by the rest of the, the men ringing handbells and if the doors were opened, um, red ribbons were tied on to the horse figure and this was to symbolise good luck and fertility. Um, later on the horse skull was stuck on to a stick and, this produced a hobby horse and this became part of the dance.

A: It, it looks so pretty when you see it because of all the ribbons, and the bells and the sticks and everything. It's very exciting, but it's very hard to understand why, you know . . .

B: Well I think, I think it's actually, I mean why, I mean . . . ultimately I think it's a very good excuse for them all to have a very good time and get very drunk . . . (*laughter*)

Unit 5   Rings on my fingers and bells on my toes

1   I never go anywhere without it
1) . . . Well, it's silver. And . . . ah . . . it's in the shape of a bee. And I, I love it. I never go anywhere without it. I used to take it off at night, I don't any more. And, um, the cats, my cats, I've got two cats, jumped up on to the table where I left it, and knocked it off onto the floor, and in between some floor boards, and I couldn't get it up. And I was very upset. So I went back to the shop where my husband bought it and ah . . . they happened to have another one, exactly the same. So . . . I bought it. And now I never never take it off in case the cats see it. (*laughter*)

2) . . . Well, I used to wear a lot of them but um . . . there was one I had um . . . and it was a great big one. It was like a . . . it was all hand hammered silver. And it had all these dents in it, and plus around the outside it had these sort of silver donuts . . . which are hammered into it as well . . . it was the most fantastic thing I had . . . and then I went to a concert in Hyde Park and I climbed a tree to . . . to, so I could get a better view, and my, somehow my hand caught on a, a twig or something and it just flew out and I could see it . . . I was about thirty feet high and it just fell straight down and I thought, 'Oh, that's no problem, I'll just get down and get it.' But I, when I got down the tree it was gone. I never found it again. Of course it was completely unique . . . so it was kind of a tragedy . . .

3) . . . I know the feeling. I had . . . um . . . I had one which was silver, and it had this huge house on it (*Mmmm*) It was like . . . a cottage. Like um . . . a fairy-tale cottage and very beautiful, but very heavy . . . But I took it off one day, um . . . to wash my hands or something and it completely disappeared. It was like it had never ever been there and I never ever found it. (*How*

horrible. How extraordinary. That's very strange. Yes. Very odd.)

4) . . . The thing that I remember so well is . . . ah . . . it's an ornament that you wear on your leg. Now you wear one on the left leg, one on the right leg. It's a . . . an ornament well known in Nigeria, for when people are happy, when you're greeting people, a certain dance is done with these things strapped to your legs. Now the particular vegetable fruit that you use for it is called the calabash. And the calabash against the gold or the silver creates a sound like a tick, tack a tack a doo . . . And this is the particular Nigerian ornament.

Unit 6   Concrete jungles?

4   What an experience!
A: I used to live in London . . . And, um . . . have I ever been frightened at night? Yes, I was, when I . . . if I came home late from the theatre on my own, I used to be quite scared, um . . . because the streets were deserted and you did hear of . . . ah, people being attacked late at night. So I used to walk up the middle of the street very noisily and very fast, ha . . . and whistling to keep myself happy. Ah . . . but I never saw anybody. And, ah . . .

B: It must have worked.

A: Oh yes, it did, it certainly did. (*laughs*)

B: Mm. I think the, the time, ah . . . that I was most in danger and was most frightened, was in a very unexpected place. It was in my family's home town, which is Austin, in Texas . . . One night, ah . . . my brother and I were walking down the main drag in Austin – when suddenly this brawl erupted out on the street. It was absolutely terrifying to face this kind of unreasoning violence. It was absolutely terrifying. We just got out of it as soon as we could and sprinted down the street before the cops arrived.

A: Were you injured?

B: No . . . I . . . I you know I got banged on the shoulders and ah . . . but no one actually hit me in the face.

C: Um . . . I did a job in Copenhagen, a long time ago. And, ah, there, . . . nobody was on the streets at all. And I felt very safe. I always feel very safe when there's hardly anybody around. And ah . . . it was very clean, which . . . psychologically meant for me that it was very safe. And one day I was walking around like this and I hadn't realised there was um . . . a riot on. (*laughs*) um . . . a Danish riot. But, ah . . . there's a place called a walking street, which means there is no traffic on the street and I was walking down there completely alone, not a sight of anybody, and suddenly I just heard this . . . thunder, and down towards me came running hundreds of people. And, ah . . . I was just standing there with shock and they just all ran past me and then there was silence again. It was . . . very odd.

B: What was it about? Did you know?

C: Education, I think.

Unit 7   Dangerous situations

4   Got a light?

Excuse me, excuse me, yeah, yeah you . . . you got a light?

☆

Look, I, I don't want to hassle you, but, but I really need a few dollars for a meal, my welfare cheque hasn't arrived . . . just a couple of bucks . . . you know what I mean . . .

☆

You've got money, dressed like that . . . you're not poor . . . just give me a bit of cash. OK . . . and I won't hurt you . . . You start to struggle and I'll get angry . . . got it? . . . I'll hurt you . . . I need cash OK? Now . . . come on . . . give . . . now . . . understand? . . . now!

☆

OK . . . you had your chance . . . you think you can mess around with me . . . no way . . . give me all your cash . . . all of it now . . . or I'll cut you . . . and mark you real bad . . . you'll bleed real bad . . . Come on I don't have time for games . . . do it, do you hear, just do it . . . your purse, wallet or whatever . . . give it to me right now . . . Come on . . . come on . . . do it . . . you.

Unit 8   Lean on me

1   Lean on me

Sometimes in our lives we all have pain, we all have sorrow
But if we are wise, we know that there's always tomorrow.
Lean on me when you're not strong
And I'll be your friend, I'll help you carry on
For it won't be long, till I'm going to need
Somebody to lean on.

Please swallow your pride if I have faith you need to borrow
For no one can fill those of your needs that you won't let show.
You just call on me brother, when you need a hand
We all need somebody to lean on.
I just might have a problem that you'll understand
We all need somebody to lean on.

Unit 9   Just dial this number . . .

2   Telephoning for advice

Hi, this is Tom. My uncle Alex had a wooden leg. If you ever want a drawing pin, ask me, he'd say. He used to keep a lot of drawing pins, together with shopping lists and little memos, on his left ankle. That's what I call turning a minus into a plus, turning a disadvantage into an advantage. Whatever you look like, whatever disadvantages you have, be yourself. Use what you have. You'll never be a success if you're trying to be somebody else. That's like a, a teapot trying to be a lion. If you're a teapot, be the best one around. Stick to what you do, but do it well.

To be successful you must have clear goals, know what you want, have definite targets and concentrate on them. If you're relaxed and yourself, other people will like you. There's no need to pretend, ever. Just be you, yourself. Don't fear failure. You'll fail sometimes. We all do. So what? The only way never to fail is never to try anything. Use your imagination, be brave and you'll never be sorry you had a try.

Unit 11   The gift of life

6   A twist of fate

The medical scientist suddenly becomes ill again with a serious blood disorder. The scientist's family believe that the transplanted kidney is a diseased one and want to make the whole event public in an effort to find another kidney quickly. The story of the transplant gets into the papers. The surgeon refuses to admit anything. Charges of malpractice cannot be proved. A new kidney is offered to the scientist as a result of the press coverage but he dies before he can receive it. Ironically, the original kidney he received is found to be perfectly good. The little girl, still clinging grimly to life, is given the new kidney by the same surgeon. She recovers and goes on to lead a healthy life. She eventually does a Ph.D. in medical politics.

Unit 12   Winner takes all

4   I'm the world's worst gambler . . .

A: I have to say, I'm very partial to a game of poker. Um . . . I think this started when I was in the sixth form at school. That's where I learnt my skill . . . um . . . and ah, some time ago I was in Spain, staying at this hotel with a whole lot of people, and one night some of these chaps decided they would have a game of poker, and I said, 'Can I play?' and they rather, I mean, they said, 'Oh, O.K.' but they . . . they really thought I was going to hold them back a bit and wasn't going to be quite up to scratch . . . But anyway we played all night, and various amounts of money changed hands. We decided, you know, last, last hand . . . and, um . . . I had a full house and won about sixty five quid off them and they were a bit . . . fed up, really.

B: I can imagine why . . . I could be a gambler if I was more lucky, I think, or more skilled. But I'm neither. I remember my most exciting gambling was er, . . . on Sydney Harbour, where they have, (*clears his throat*) they have eighteen foot skips, which are sailing boats and all the people pack on to a ferry which goes from buoy to buoy around, around the course, and, and they have bookies downstairs and you bet on the boats and see which boats are going to win. It's a very exciting form of gambling, and at one stage I was, I was downstairs and I heard one of the bookies saying, 'Twenty to one on Travel Lodge', because it was coming tenth or something, doing very badly at this stage but it was about half way through the race. So I raced downstairs and put, ah . . . and put ten dollars on at twenty to one, and, ah, and the boat eventually, an hour later, won the race and I made more money than I've ever made gambling before.

A: How much did you make?

B: Well, twenty to one at . . . ten dollars, that's . . .

A: Two hundred and ten, you get your ten dollars back, and two hundred dollars.

C: I have to say, I'm the world's worst. I'm the unluckiest gambler (*laughter*). I mean I don't win, I don't win raffles at the village fete, and if I ever get a sweepstake ticket on the Grand National or something the horse falls over (*laughter*) and has to be shot . . . I was once in Monte Carlo with a group of people, we were working there and, ah . . . the other guys were all saying, 'Ah, come on, come on, we'll all go to the Casino tonight . . .' I said, 'No, no I won't, I can't go' and they said, 'No, no, come on' . . . and they went and I had a little, tiny flutter and it was disaster, I was losing all the time, but they discovered that if they stood me next to people who were winning, their luck changed and my friends (*laughter*) started winning themselves. (*laughter*) So that . . . the winner at the table . . . because I was just standing near them, seemed to start losing and my friends started winning.

A: Well, just never sit next to me when I'm playing poker.

Unit 13   A roll of the dice

1   Shall I stay or shall I go?

You are on a ship. You are standing on the deck looking down at a small boat. In the boat are the ship's captain and some of the sailors. Behind you are other sailors who have taken control of the ship because they hated the cruel captain. You did not take part in the mutiny but you have to decide: are you going to go with the captain or are you going to stay with the men on the ship?

If you go with the captain, you will be in a small boat in dangerous seas, thousands of kilometres from home. The captain has shown that he is harsh and cruel. You may all die. But if you survive, you will arrive home to a hero's welcome.

If you stay with the men on the ship, you will sail to a beautiful island and start a completely new life. But you will never be able to go back to your own country and you will never see your family and friends again.

6   Reporting back

1 You must prepare for a journey of self discovery. You must leave friends and loved ones within 30 days and journey to a far land. You must enter the lives of three people in that land and help them to survive and live a fruitful life.

2 You must exchange lives with another

person in your class. For a period of three months you will live his or her life and he or she will live your life. The exchange must be complete.

3 You must give up life as you now know it and join the tramps and vagrants in the city. You must participate fully in their lives and use the wisdom that you gain in your own life. You must live as a street dweller for one year.

4 You must first fly in balloons, gliders, and hang gliders. Feel like a bird, free in the air. From this freedom in the skies you must learn the value of space and spend three months alone in a dark underground cave with only candles, books, food and drink. This is your chance to test your strength of character and to conquer loneliness.

5 You must go to live among wild animals. Study them, learn their ways, live as they do. You must not speak your own language or read or listen to it for a period of six months but you can imitate the call of the animals.

6 You will receive a large amount of money. You must spend it all on yourself during a period of two months. Even if you are tempted to give things to others, you must resist. Indulge yourself in all those ways you have dreamt of but never thought possible, but do so alone. You must not share your fortune with anyone.

Unit 14   What's on tonight?

2   Movie talk

Mine is um, I think a sort of American film. And that is um . . . *A Woman on the Edge.* (*ah yes*) And, um . . . it's a John Cassavetes film, and it is largely improvised. And the actors in it are just wonderful. It's about a woman on the edge of a nervous breakdown. Um, she drinks too much, she has a controlling husband, and her children are deeply disturbed.

Ah, I see. Ahhh . . . Well my film is more about love, I keep seeing often and often again, it's called *Les Enfants du Paradis.* (*Oh yeah, yeah . . .*) It's a film in the 1940s, ah, a film made in the French industry during the time of occupation. What I loved about it, they had mime . . . they had a wonderful lead actress called Arletty. But it was a film about love, the

highest ideals of love, in Paris, the time of the nineteenth century. And set in a theatre. And about all the life that goes on outside of the theatre, in the streets, and what happens in order to get a theatre going every night.

Unit 16   Have you got Mexican red-knees?

2   She's an absolute pet!

Interviewer: So, can you tell me when your passion for these pets began?

Woman: Mm, well, it started when we bought our first one, really . . . Um we bought a Mexican red-knee, which is probably the one that everybody thinks of. And . . . once you start, you really don't know where to stop. (*laughs*)

Int: And these animals, how would you describe them, as pets?

W: Oh, they are to me . . . yeah, they're all part of my family, so therefore they're all pets.

Int: Right, well, can you introduce me to some of them?

W: I certainly will. Well, we'll start with this one, this is Annie. She's my favourite. She's about eight, she's a real sweetie, she's an absolute poppet. She's very docile, she's actually very, very friendly.

Int: And how, how can you tell that she's a female?

W: It's not easy, actually. By her age, that's the best way to tell. And if you look at this little chap here, you can see him . . .

Int: And this is a male, is it?

W: That is a male. And you can see, he's got little tiny hooks on his legs, you see them?

Int: Mmm I see, yes.

W: And he's actually quite a small male . . . just there, you see, those little hooks? See them?

Int: Yes, yes I do.

W: Now, he's a male.

Int: What . . . er, what is it they feed on?

W: Well, they feed on live insects, which maybe is a thing that puts a lot of people from keeping them, really . . .

Int: (*nervous giggle*) So when . . . er, when is feeding time?

W: Well, we feed ours once a week. Because that's really all they need.

Int: Right. Right. And . . . um . . . is it . . . is it possible or is it wise for you to take one out?

W: Yes, do you want to hold one? If . . . look, I'll take Annie out for you.
Int: Hm . . . um . . . yes, well, you, you just set her down there . . . and . . . I . . .
W: Here she is.
Int: I'll sit back.
W: I'll set her down here, all right?
Int: Um, let me just, let me just describe to the listeners, as, as you're about to do it. She . . . she hasn't reacted at all, has . . . oh, oh, yes, yes, she's, she's lifted a leg, that is a leg . . .
W: That is a leg. She's actually probably asleep, so she's not best pleased with me. I'm going to wake her up for you.
W: Yes . . . Come on, sweetie . . . Come on, love . . .
Int: And she lifts her front legs and you're, you're putting your hand underneath her . . .
W: That's a good girl.
Int: And . . . picking her up. And . . . oh, and she's, she's covering both hands, and . . . and the legs . . . and, and . . . feeling all round.
W: There you go. And that's Annie, look. And she's my pet.
Int: What do you actually get from a moment like this, when you're . . . you're sitting holding Annie.
W: Mm, well, probably sounds silly, but I love my pets. To me, they are beautiful . . . and they are graceful. Just look at her. Now of course, most people would be absolutely terrified.
Int: Wi . . . with some justification.
W: No, no, no. There is not one of these in the world that will kill a human being. They're not naturally aggressive . . . towards anything, not even humans. Oh, they'll grab their food but to human beings or people dealing with them, they are not aggressive.
Int: Good. Now . . . um . . . let's put it back in the cage, shall we?

Unit 18   Good fences make good neighbours

3   It was such a nice neighbourhood!
I actually live at the moment in Bayswater which is an area of London. And, um . . . it is changing very rapidly there. And at the moment what is happening is that, um . . . we have had a new shop in the area. The shop has only opened in the last few months. Um . . . what is

happening is that, the first thing that has happened is that yellow lines – so you can't park – have appeared in Queensway which annoys everybody because we could park before to do our food shopping. And now to park you have to pay a great deal of money in the car park. Ah . . . the other thing that is happening is that the prices of the houses are actually going up again at a time when they have been going down. And, ah . . . this is affecting the community. The community is very mixed, racially, and very mixed, ah . . . economically. And, ah . . . but what is good is that because there is a large Arab population and because their demand is for late night shopping, the shops are open seven days a week and till nine or ten o'clock at night. So that's not too bad. And there are more trees now. But on the other hand . . . um . . . there are more beggars on the street and more drunks on the street. So part of it is good and part of it is bad.

Well, all those problems that you've just mentioned, Suhad, are very much affecting Calabar at the moment. I mean, it was always a neighbourhood of village people speaking different languages coming together. But because of the new sort of life being introduced in the Crosswood estates area of Calabar, it means the motorway has had to be included and this means clearing away the swamp areas, clearing away the trees – the palm trees, the rubber trees, all the natural flora and all the land that the local people used to work on and till to get their food has become now land in the hands of the property developers. And . . . it's not the place that I remember. And to the extent that the local rainfall has changed now, the area has become a little drier than before . . . (*Mm*) And when you're very much dependent on seasons, and dry season or wet season, and it's not as wet as it used to be, that is a serious problem . . .

Unit 19   Boundary disputes

2   The answerphone message
Ah, hello, this is . . . ah, Pete Bargello. I'm your neighbour on the south side. I see you're beginning to dig the end of your garden . . . ah, the one closest to my property. Um . . . I don't know why you're doing that – I mean, that part of the garden belongs to me, you must realise. I . . . I bought it five years ago from the guy who

was here before, Mr Leckie. And I paid good money for it. I haven't done much with it, OK, OK, but but it's mine. You must have noticed there's no fence between that bit and . . . and my own garden. So would you please keep to your side of the garden, OK? I mean, I've asked my . . . my builder to come in and he's going to put up a wire fence just to make sure that everyone's perfectly clear which bit is yours and which bit is mine, OK? Just stay your side of the fence and I'm sure we'll get on just fine.

3 Prompt action

Hello, it's me. Guess what that Bargello guy has done? He's put up a wire fence already, so now we can't get to the bottom of our garden. I'm so angry! On top of that, he's pulled out four of the young trees we planted as well! What are we going to do now? . . . Look, I've got to dash. I'll see you later and we'll talk about it then. OK? Bye.

Unit 20 Memorials

2 They were just getting to the most difficult part . . .

1 In the days before the Bay Bridge was built, there was a ferry to take people across the Bay to Sydney itself. Now Jack Smith was very well known in those days. He used to come over on the ferry every evening to drink in the various bars and cafes, and he was one of those people that, you know, everyone knows and loves, because he was pretty funny, you know, especially when he'd had a few pints. Well one day there was very thick . . . um, you know, fog as the ferry set out. There was Jack sitting on the deck as usual, with his bottle, already feeling quite merry. But suddenly, there was this really loud crash as the ferry struck a rock and . . .

2 Lord McAlroy was a wealthy land owner in this area. That was in the . . . the eighteenth century, I think. In those days, rich lords thought they could do just about anything, and Lord McAlroy was always in the local inn boasting about everything that he could do. He was especially keen on his horses. Well, one night some people were listening to him going on about his marvellous horse and all he could do with it, and they said just quietly, like, they didn't think anyone could ride all the way up the steep ridge of the nearest

mountain. Well, you can imagine, there was no stopping him then. The next day he set off with his poor horse, in the wind and the rain, on this terrible steep path. Now, just as they were getting to the most difficult part . . .

3 Hans Wellen was always a lively youngster, but he couldn't fit into an ordinary school – his sense of fun just landed him into trouble, time and time and time again. When he was a teenager, though, he went with a school party into the Alps and was introduced to rope climbing and that's when he really found his own way in life. After that, he couldn't get into trouble again, because he didn't have time – he was too busy climbing. As soon as he could leave school, he got a job as a caretaker in a hotel in the mountains. One day, some young South Americans were staying in the hotel, and they asked him to take them up to the highest slopes for some skiing. The weather wasn't very good, but . . .

3 Visiting the Peace Gardens in Hiroshima

Ladies and gentlemen, we are now entering the Peace Memorial Park. The monuments and museum here are dedicated to stopping nuclear war: 'No More Hiroshimas'. If you look straight ahead, you will see the Atom Bomb Dome. That's the first thing visitors see when they come here. It's a powerful symbol. When the bomb exploded at 8.15 a.m. on August 6 1945, two hundred thousand people died. And as you know, more than half the city was destroyed. But the building which was directly under the bomb didn't collapse completely. It was the Industrial Promotion Hall, but it is now the Atom Bomb Dome – it's half shattered as you can see but it still stands – the only ruin of the war which is still left in Hiroshima. Now as we walk across the bridge, we can see the Peace Memorial Museum straight ahead of us at the far end of the park. (*fade*)
Now we have come to the other side of the park. Here in front of us is the statue to all the children who died because of the atom bomb. You can see it shows a young girl who died of atomic radiation. She wanted to live very, very much. She thought that if she made 1000 paper birds, she would live. But when she had made 954, she died . . . Now ladies and gentlemen, please follow me, and we'll go (*fade*)

To the teacher

This book has been written to encourage the development of fluency in spoken English. It is intended for students who have reached an upper-intermediate level. Having built a secure foundation of grammatical forms and vocabulary, learners at this level have more resources with which to express their own thoughts and feelings. However, they still need to build their confidence and sense of ease in the new language if they are to become able to associate English with a richer representation of their own personalities.

Developing fluency implies taking risks, letting go safely by using language in a relaxed, friendly atmosphere – an atmosphere of trust and support. Speaking fluently implies being able to communicate easily and appropriately with others. In the classroom, this can best be achieved if teacher and learners share a belief that says 'what you are saying is more important to me than how accurately you are saying it'. This belief validates the speaker first and foremost as a person rather than as a producer of correctly formed utterances.

The format of *Speaking 3* is slightly different from that used in the earlier books of the series. Firstly, some units suggest group projects that take students out of the classroom, for example on a fun walk or to the cinema. Occasionally a class exhibition or poster display is suggested as feedback and talking point. Clearly, these projects will be ideal for some classes but not suitable for others, and teachers will choose accordingly. Our own experience is that this type of activity often works surprisingly well, even with unlikely classes, producing tangible benefits in the form of increased student solidarity.

Secondly, a number of units in the latter part of the book are thematically paired (units 12/13, 14/15, 16/17 and 18/19). The first unit in each pair contains varied activities based on one theme. These can be used individually or combined in any way which suits particular classes and learning situations. They can also serve as warm-up activities to lead into the following unit. The second unit in each pair is built around the same broad theme as the first, but is different in format. It consists of an integrated, extended activity, divided into parts, to be used in the sequence suggested. More time may therefore have to be set aside for the second unit in each pair. Although some preparatory work can occasionally be done by students at home, the group activities in the classroom will normally fill the whole of one or even two periods. Some of these integrated units offer what is essentially a simulation: that is, learners are asked to imagine that they are part of an ongoing situation and to respond to it with their own thoughts and decisions.

The simulations have been designed to be accessible to upper-intermediate level students. The amount of text to be read and assimilated has been kept fairly low, and some of the information needed to set up the situations is given in the form of listening material on the cassette.

It has been our aim in these integrated units to encourage the student to use language in a context which is more demanding. In this case 'demanding' means that the student has the opportunity for more extended verbal interaction with others either because the core situation is an unfolding one, or because the unit involves a moral or social dilemma.

The cassette

You will find the materials available on the cassette marked by ▭. We believe that an ability to deal with unsimplified spoken English is a vital accompaniment to the development of spoken fluency. However, in order to avoid overburdening the students' capacities for comprehension, many of our listening tasks require understanding only at the level of gist.

As in the earlier books, the listening materials are of several types. Some of the materials have accompanying gist comprehension tasks, for example, matching exercises, note taking or retelling the main points. There are some music based listening activities and most listening pieces lead learners naturally on to making spoken comparisons with their own situation. In this book there is also another type of listening. In the units with simple simulations, listening extracts comprise part of the action, part of the 'event', and are thus integral. These extracts sometimes require more detailed comprehension.

Where listening tasks have specific answers, these can be found in the tapescript.

The listening materials in this book include speakers from a variety of nations and thus provide a rich base for the comprehension of spoken English.

Grading

We have tried to order the twenty units in such a way that the more straightforward ones are earliest in the sequence, but there has been no conscious linguistic grading. Within each unit there are activities which pose varying degrees of challenge to the linguistic resources of the student. Teachers, no doubt, will make selections and adaptations accordingly.

Students working together

All our units invite students to talk with one another in small groups or in pairs. Being in a classroom learning a language is essentially a social experience and should be memorable, in part, because of the relationships forged during a time of being and learning together. In fluency work one of our aims is to make learners less conscious of their vulnerability in the target language by tempting them to become interested in the people in the classroom and therefore more willing to take risks to satisfy their curiosity.

Encouraging fluency in the classroom

Fluency materials, especially those that explore personal topics, rely on the skill of the teacher in easing students into the themes and in setting an atmosphere of trust and respect. Sensitivity to the needs and desires of a particular class becomes more important than ever when teachers come to select a theme or unit and begin to orient their students to it. It is vital that the topic should intrigue and engage students so that they are keen to share their own ideas and feelings about it with others in the group.

In piloting this material, we found that some classes responded very positively to what might be considered rather serious issues, organ transplants, for example, while others were not in the mood for them. The last unit which raises the issue of remembering and commemorating might be avoided if students have been recently bereaved. The teacher is best placed to find and choose the right material for particular students. Nevertheless, we hope that the units in this book will provide enough variety to enable teachers to find suitable material for different types of classes.

The preliminary care needed to choose appropriate themes and to create a classroom atmosphere that is relaxed and supportive is probably useful for most areas of language work – but where the aim is specifically to foster fluency, it is indispensable. Whereas learners can attain accuracy by doing a series of exercises in step with others in the class, they are unlikely to become more fluent unless they 'do their own thing' and become motivated to communicate something of their own thoughts and experiences. Talking about topics in which they take a personal interest and about which they care allows them to associate their new language with their own lives, and this is particularly important when the learners are learning English in their own country. It also strengthens and enriches the quality of social contact in the classroom and widens the boundaries of interaction involving the target language.

Practice of particular areas of language

In this book, we have decided not to include as many lists of useful language as in *Speaking 1* and *Speaking 2* and we have not explicitly encouraged overt

practice of particular phrases or forms. Our assumptions are that:
— learners at the upper-intermediate level have already acquired a
  foundation of language forms, functions and vocabulary but may still lack
  fluency in using them.
— learners may still be using a core coursebook that gives them enough
  conventional presentation and practice of particular forms and functions.
Teachers monitor their learners constantly and can judge when certain
areas of language are either missing or in need of repair. These judgements
will form the basis for follow-up language work tailored by teachers to their
particular learners. Our decision is consistent with what has been termed a
'bottom up' approach. This implies that much more room is left for teachers
to make their own decisions on precisely what areas of language their
learners need to work on, and how to approach that work. Fluency materials
allow students to pull out of their memory, and recycle, some of the
vocabulary or forms they have learned in their main coursework and at the
same time give teachers an ideal opportunity to monitor this process of
language activation.

We believe that at the upper-intermediate level, students can augment their
proficiency at using conversational devices and vocabulary as much by
listening to fairly authentic examples of spoken English as by studying such
language in written form. The extracts on the cassette provide help in these
endeavours. Students also get reinforcement of spoken discourse from each
other in their group activities.

Inexperienced teachers

We encourage teachers who have had little teaching experience or little
experience of materials like these to be bold in selecting activities and ideas
from this book and adapting them to their teaching styles and to the type of
classes and students that they have. The book provides a framework only,
and experiment is sometimes the only way to find the most suitable methods
or materials for particular learners.

Cultural location

Our material tries to cast a wide geographical net rather than be centred
exclusively in British or other English-speaking locations. In many of the
units students are asked to talk in English about their home towns, villages
or cities, or about the environment in which they are now living. This seems
consistent with a belief that students can talk more easily and flexibly about
places they know well.

We wish you an interesting and fruitful time with the activities in this book and
welcome comments and reactions from teachers who use these materials.